M.L.S.
BETWEEN &
PH.D.

A Study of Sixth-Year
Specialist Programs in
Accredited Library Schools

J. Periam Danton

American Library Association
Chicago 1970

International Standard Book Number 0-8389-0089-5 (1970)
Library of Congress Catalog Card Number 74-133380
Printed in the United States of America

Contents

Figures

Tables

Preface

The intent of this survey is to describe educational practice (to spring 1969) in the emerging sixth-year specialist programs in library schools accredited by the American Library Association. The study, carried out under the sponsorship of the Committee on Accreditation of the American Library Association, was made possible by a J. Morris Jones—World Book Encyclopedia—ALA Goals Award, established by Field Enterprises Educational Corporation.

From the time that Lester Asheim, Director of the ALA Office for Library Education, first approached me on behalf of the committee to undertake this study, my assignment has been interesting and challenging. I am grateful to the committee for entrusting the study to me, and for the opportunity of serving the committee, library education, and, perhaps to some extent, the profession at large.

I should like to express here, also, my thanks to those who have assisted me and have helped to make the study possible. First among these are the deans/directors and faculty members of the library schools, whose fullest cooperation has made prosecution of the study a pleasant task. Without the help, especially, of the deans and directors, all of whom spent a good deal of time in supplying essential information, the study would quite clearly have been impossible. The profession owes a substantial debt to them. Dr. Asheim's constant advice, assistance, and encouragement were a source of great satisfaction to me. Dr. Agnes Reagan, Assistant Director for Accreditation, in the ALA Office for Library Education; Dr. Margaret Monroe, Dean of the Library School, University of

Wisconsin; and Dr. Asheim, were most helpful in providing me with comment and criticism on various drafts of the questionnaires for the schools and their graduates. I am also grateful to Dr. Asheim, Dr. Reagan, and my wife for valuable suggestions on a draft of the manuscript. Finally, I owe special thanks to the research assistant on the project, Mrs. Jovana Brown, who shared the library school visits with me, assisted in the design and construction of the questionnaires, and performed most of the labor of tabulation, statistical analysis, and chart design; Mr. William Brown, who drew the maps; Mr. Robert Remen, who constructed the graphs; Miss Aili Sargent, who handled all the correspondence and other clerical chores; and Mrs. Hedwig Doehring, who typed the final versions of the study.

Because of the sponsorship of this work by a committee of ALA, I might note that responsibility for its findings is solely mine. It is in no sense an official statement of the Committee on Accreditation, and none of the views expressed necessarily represent the opinion of the committee or the American Library Association.

J. P. D.

| Chapter 1 | # Background of the Sixth-Year Specialist Program |

The first formal program of library education in the United States was established at Columbia College (now University) in 1887. In the following thirty-five years more than a dozen additional schools were founded, some in large public libraries, some in schools of technology, a few in universities.

Williamson's seminal, now-famous study of library education in the United States covered fifteen programs, only eight of them associated with institutions of higher education.[1] There were no standards, and the several programs, varying considerably from institution to institution but in general of poor quality, were under no sort of overall supervision or control.

A major and pervasive recommendation of Williamson's report was for the creation of a national standardizing and accrediting agency.[2] The American Library Association implemented this recommendation in 1924 by establishing the Board of Education for Librarianship (B.E.L.).[3]

In the statement of standards which appeared in its First

[1] Charles C. Williamson, *Training for Library Service: A Report Prepared for the Carnegie Corporation of New York* (New York, 1923). The study was authorized in 1919, and Williamson visited the schools in 1920 - 21.

[2] Ibid., p.121 ff. and 145.

[3] *ALA Bulletin* 19: 226 (July 1925).

Annual Report, the B.E.L. had made a place for library schools which would grant a master's degree upon the completion of two years of postbaccalaureate education, that is, a degree for an advanced program beyond the basic degree.[4] Under the provision of these standards, five schools were accredited to award advanced degrees: California, Chicago, Columbia, Illinois, and Michigan.[5] Illinois, the first to do so, began in 1927; Michigan later in the same year; California and Columbia in 1928; and Chicago (which in its early years had no basic, first-year curriculum) late in 1928. Carroll has determined that between 1927 and 1960 the five schools awarded 1,451 of these "sixth-year" master's degrees.[6] He also points out the less-well-known fact that six other schools, besides the five specifically accredited to do so, had advanced programs for which master's degrees were occasionally awarded. These six were: Drexel, Louisiana, McGill, Peabody, Toronto, and Western Reserve; among them, through 1960, they awarded forty-five degrees.[7] It is reasonably certain that these programs, providing additional education beyond the single year which was the basic requirement for entrance to the profession, were library education's response to the need felt by many larger libraries for staff members with more intensive and comprehensive professional education than could be secured in the single year. The list of schools offering advanced programs remained unchanged for two decades.

Meanwhile, in 1933, all library schools were reclassified in conformity with the Minimum Requirements for Library Schools adopted by the Council of the American Library

[4] Ibid., p.246.

[5] Throughout this work the library schools mentioned are referred to by their common, abbreviated names, the full names being given in Appendix A. Thus "Pittsburgh" equals Graduate School of Library and Information Sciences, University of Pittsburgh; "Illinois" equals Graduate School of Library Science, University of Illinois; and "Western Michigan" equals Department of Librarianship, Western Michigan University.

[6] Carmal Edward Carroll, "The Professionalization of Education for Librarianship, with Special Reference to the Years 1940 - 1960" (Ph.D. dissertation, Univ. of California, 1969), p.262.

[7] Ibid.

2

Association at the Fifty-fifth Annual Conference.[8] At this time there were twenty-seven accredited schools, twenty-six in the United States and one in Canada. Fifteen of them, classified Type III, offered a year of library education within the four-year undergraduate college program; seven, classified Type II, offered a year of library education, but required college graduation for admission; and five schools, already named and designated Type I, required college graduation for admission and, in addition, were accredited for advanced study. This pattern of library education remained unchanged for almost fifteen years.[9]

In 1947, the Board of Education for Librarianship, influenced at least in part by the severe shortage of librarians caused by the war and the inflation following it, made a great break with tradition by approving a University of Denver plan for a program leading, at the end of *one* postbaccalaureate year, to a master's degree, and the B.E.L. issued a statement which encouraged similar experimentation in the other schools.[10] By this time the number of accredited schools had increased to thirty-seven—a 37 percent increase in fewer than fifteen years—of which two were Canadian. The same five schools were still Type I, and there were nineteen Type II and thirteen Type III schools.

Both before and after the B.E.L.'s action considerable opposition to the new scheme was evident.[11] "A question-

[8] *ALA Bulletin* 27: 431 - 32, 610 - 13 (15 December 1933).

[9] Ibid., 28: H321 - H322 (November 1934).

[10] Ibid., 41: 378 - 79 (15 October 1947). A full account of the history of American library education (to ca. 1951), including the developments relevant to this discussion, may be found in Alice I. Bryan, *The Public Librarian* (New York: Columbia Univ. Pr., 1952), p.299 - 451. A history of the most recent period may be found in Carmal Edward Carroll, op. cit. See also Sarah K. Vann, *Training for Librarianship before 1923: Education for Librarianship Prior to the Publication of Williamson's Report on Training for Library Service* (Chicago: American Library Assn., 1961); Carl Milton White, *The Origins of the American Library School* (New York: Scarecrow, 1961); Louis Round Wilson, "Historical Development of Education for Librarianship in the United States," in Bernard Berelson, ed., *Education for Librarianship* (Chicago: American Library Assn., 1949).

[11] See, e.g., J. Periam Danton, "This Curriculum Business," *Library Journal* 73: 1126, 1174 - 75 (1 September 1948); Harold Lancour,

naire sent to the accredited library schools by a joint commit-tee of the B.E.L. and the Association of American Library Schools in 1944 ... with regard to granting the master's degree at the end of five years of liberal arts and professional training, encountered an overwhelmingly negative re-sponse."[12] Opposition continued after the approval of the Denver program, chiefly on the grounds that (a) numbers of librarians with more than a single year of professional educa-tion were needed, and (b) the awarding of a master's degree at the end of five years of liberal arts and professional educa-tion would operate like a kind of Gresham's law to drive out the advanced programs which awarded a master's degree at the end of six years of post-high school education. Despite the opposition, however, it soon became clear that programs like Denver's were the wave of the future; by the early 1950s, when the schools were being reevaluated under new standards for accreditation adopted in 1951, most library schools had converted, and by 1955 all had done so.[13] Cali-fornia was the last school to conform to the new order of things.

It also shortly became clear that the major fear of those who had opposed that order was justified. The awarding of a master's degree at the end of the fifth year of post-high school education made unviable master's degree programs that required an additional year of study. By 1957 the sixth-year master's programs in the United States were no longer enrolling students, and by 1960, when the last degree appears to have been awarded, these programs were a thing of the past. California, again, was the last school to surrender.

The basic structure, now, of library education remained unchanged for another half-dozen years: entry into the pro-fession required five years of post-high school education, the award for which was the (new) master's degree; and a small but increasing number of schools had programs leading to the doctorate. By and large, there was no halfway house. But by

"Presidential Address," Association of American Library Schools, *Report of Meeting*, 1 February 1956, p.5.

[12] Bryan, op. cit., p.325.

[13] *ALA Bulletin* 46: 48 - 49 (February 1952). Classification by type—I, II, and III—was abandoned at this time.

1962, after a history of thirty-three years, all the seven schools which then had doctoral programs had graduated only 173 individuals.[14]

Even with the establishment of doctoral programs in additional schools (there was a total of thirteen in June 1969; two others began in September) and the considerable increase in the numbers of doctoral students, particularly with the availability of substantial fellowships under Title II-B of the Higher Education Act of 1965, it was apparent to many in the profession, first, that the number of doctoral graduates would never be sufficient to fill the needs of larger libraries for personnel with specialized knowledge and more-than-minimal professional education; and, second, that the steadily enlarging demands which our very rapidly changing society was placing upon librarians and libraries were calling for more people with professional education beyond the one-year M.L.S. degree.

This was the situation when, in 1961, the library school at Columbia University established the first of what have now come to be known as "sixth-year specialist programs" (sometimes abbreviated s.y.s.ps.), that is, programs involving a year of "specialized" study beyond the M.L.S. degree. These programs appeared to be similar in several respects to those of the "old," sixth-year master's degree. There is, in fact, a kind of merging or overlapping of the two: the antecedent of Peabody's present program was begun in 1954, suspended in 1965, and finally reinstated in 1968; Toronto inaugurated a program for a sixth-year master's degree in 1950, when five U.S. schools also had such programs. By late 1967 it was known that programs of this general nature had been established in at least eleven schools, although no list, or even partial list, had been published.[15] In one important respect the new specialist programs differ from the "old" sixth-year

[14] J. Periam Danton, "Doctoral Study in Librarianship in the United States," *College and Research Libraries* 20: 435 - 53, 458 (November 1959); and J. Periam Danton and LeRoy C. Merritt, "Doctoral Study in Librarianship—A Supplement," *College and Research Libraries* 23: 539 - 40 (November 1962).

[15] Floyd N. Fryden, "Post-Master's Degree Programs in Some American Library Schools" (unpublished paper, Graduate Library School, Univ. of Chicago, 19 March 1968). Mr. Fryden's paper, here-

master's degree—the latter was a general, across-the-board advanced curriculum; the former are primarily, and almost without exception, intended to provide preparation for a particular (specialized) kind of professional activity.

The difference may be related to the fact that the period during which the old sixth-year master's degree began was a more stable, much less rapidly changing one than that of the 1960s. Whether libraries today also need employees with a general, across-the-board advanced curriculum may be moot and, in any case, is not here in question. What seems clear is that developments in information science and the concept of the instructional media center do call for specialized professional education.

It was about this time (1967) that the Committee on Accreditation (C.O.A.)—the successor of the B.E.L.—interested itself in the question of the nature, purposes, curricula, and achievements of these programs and an evaluation of their place in the overall structure of American library education. Consequently, in February 1968, a grant application bearing the following heading was prepared: "Evaluation of Specialist Programs in Librarianship: A Proposal for a Study Submitted by the Committee on Accreditation for Consideration for a J. Morris Jones—World Book Encyclopedia—ALA Goals Award." The first paragraph of the proposal read:

> This proposed study is designed to furnish a brief historical perspective on the emerging programs of specialist study in librarianship at post-master's level, to provide a summary of current programs and plans for such programs within the group of ALA-accredited library schools, and to analyze the potential of these programs in relation to the needs of the profession.

The award was made, the writer accepted the assignment of director of the project in September 1968, and preliminary work was begun in December of that year.

after cited simply as "Fryden," appeared in a slightly revised version with the title, "Post-Master's Degree Programs in the Accredited U.S. Library Schools," in *Library Quarterly* 39: 233 - 44 (July 1969), and page references throughout this study are to the published paper. The author of this study gratefully acknowledges his indebtedness to Mr. Fryden's work.

| Chapter 2 | # Scope and Method
of the Study |
| --- | --- |

Aside from Fryden's paper, no study relevant to the present one has been made. A few articles, noted in the Selected Bibliography at the end of this book, treat of the desirability of the kind of program under consideration here, the possible aims and curricula of such programs, the purposes they might achieve, or the developments in a specific school.

Definition of Terms

The principal term to be defined is the controlling one in the title of the study, "Sixth-Year Specialist Programs," and the problem of definition lies in determining when a group of courses available to qualified holders of the M.L.S. degree becomes a "program." Most of the larger and stronger schools accept library school graduates for further study on an individual, more or less ad hoc basis, even when the schools have no formal program. For the purposes of this study, a "sixth-year specialist program" is deemed to be in effect if a school has somewhat formally established a plan or program, has given it a label, has stated a purpose or purposes, and has set up requirements for admission to and completion of the work.

The definition is interpreted liberally rather than otherwise to include three schools which, though they had no "specific sixth-year curriculum" or "formal sixth-year program," nonetheless admit or admitted post-M.L.S. students on a formal basis, under clearly defined conditions, for a year of individually arranged study. It is believed that this inclusion more nearly gives a picture of the total post-M.L.S., predoctoral situation than would adherence to a more strict definition. More objective support for this view is provided by the fact that fifteen of the nineteen U.S. schools have (or had) federal support for their programs, usually through fellowships under Title II-B of the Higher Education Act of 1965. The circumstance that these schools have made formal application and received funds for their sixth-year activities suggests institutional awareness and commitment—and federal recognition.

A somewhat comparable, troublesome point of definition concerns some of the Canadian library schools. There are seven altogether, of which four—British Columbia, McGill, Toronto, and Western Ontario—are accredited. British Columbia offers a bachelor's degree only, Toronto offers both a B.L.S. and a M.L.S. program, Western Ontario has a three-semester master's program, and McGill has a M.L.S. program which requires two years for completion.[1] The programs at British Columbia and Western Ontario clearly do not concern us here. The two-year program at McGill, although it probably achieves in its second year some of the purposes of sixth-year specialist programs, cannot successfully be studied, since the two years are an integral, undifferentiated whole. This leaves Toronto, which it was decided to include on the ground that the sixth-year M.L.S. program is of the same general sort and intended for the same general purposes as are the sixth-year specialist programs in the American schools.

As a final point of "definition," it may be noted that the standards under which library schools are now accredited by the American Library Association, through the instrument of the C.O.A., were adopted in 1951.[2] Since then, the schools have not been classified by type, as was formerly the case.

---

[1] See the comprehensive and detailed article by Brian Land, "New Directions in Education for Librarianship in Canada," *Canadian Library Journal* 26: 36 - 40 (January-February 1969).

[2] *ALA Bulletin* 46: 48 - 49 (February 1952).

Methodology

The study was designed to proceed in eight steps:

1. A letter was sent to the eleven schools included in Fryden asking whether they would be willing (a) to correct and bring up to date the information relating to them which appeared in his tables; and (b) to respond to a supplementary questionnaire. Affirmative replies were received from all.

2. At the same time, a letter was sent to the remaining thirty-four accredited schools (as of spring 1969 there were forty-five accredited schools, forty-one in the United States and four in Canada), asking them if they had specialist programs and, if so, whether they would be willing to fill out a questionnaire on the subject. Replies were received from all the schools, and from these replies it was determined that nine additional schools had, or had had, specialist programs. It may be noted that three of these—Chicago, Kent, and Peabody—began, or recommenced, too recently to have been included in Fryden's study. It should also be noted that three of the twenty schools maintained their specialist programs for only a year or two and, by 1968-69, had given them up, at least temporarily. These schools are Drexel, Louisiana, and Maryland.

3. A questionnaire (Appendix B) was, in the meantime, designed, tested, revised, and sent to the nine schools not included in Fryden's study. A shortened form, omitting questions on points for which Fryden had compiled and tabulated data, was sent to the eleven schools he studied. Questionnaires from all twenty schools were in hand by the end of April.

4. One question to both groups of schools asked for the names and addresses of those who had graduated from the sixth-year specialist programs. All schools which had had graduates complied, and a total of 196 names was received from fourteen schools. As of December 1968, Atlanta, Chicago, Drexel, Kent, Rutgers, and Wayne State had had no graduates. A

questionnaire and covering letter (Appendix C) were sent during April, May, and early June to 191 of these individuals for whom effective addresses were available. Follow-up letters to nonrespondents were sent about a month after the first request. The inquiry evoked an unusually lively response as evidenced by the 82.2 percent return; by the fact that substantially more than half of the respondents provided supplementary comment and opinion, often running to two or three pages; and by the further fact that, although the questionnaire suggested that respondents might omit their names if they wished, only eleven—about 7 percent—failed to identify themselves.

5. Visits to most of the schools still operating programs were arranged and made. Four schools were visited in March, six in April, and four in June. The purpose of these visits, which were preceded by careful scrutiny of the data and opinions provided in the questionnaires, was to seek clarification or amplification of points therein, to discuss the programs informally with the deans/directors and faculty members of the schools, and to gain some sense of the programs by considering them in situ.

6. Analysis and tabulation of the returns from the schools and the graduates were begun in May and June, respectively.

7. A letter (Appendix D) was sent in July to seventy identifiable employers of eighty-three graduates.

8. Preliminary parts of the report were begun in June, and most of it was written in July. A prior commitment of the investigator to an assignment in Europe in August necessitated postponement of final drafting and completion of the report until September.

Chapter 3

The Schools

Origin and Location

Twenty schools have, or have had, sixth-year specialist programs, or, as at Toronto, a program more or less comparable in purpose leading to a sixth-year M.L.S. degree. The twenty, with the beginning dates of the sixth-year plans, are shown in table 1, and their locations in figure 1. The salient facts which the table and the figure make clear are that all but two schools, Texas and UCLA, lie east of the Mississippi; that the entire northwestern half of the country lacks a program; and that three-quarters of the schools began their programs after 1965. Only three began before 1963. The possible relationship between the beginning dates of the fifteen schools whose plans were not put into effect until 1966 or later, and the availability of support funds from the Department of Health, Education, and Welfare (HEW), via Title II-B of the Higher Education Act of 1965, is considered later. The fact that most programs are of recent date must be borne in mind in connection with some of the findings of the study, such as the relatively small number of students and graduates.

It is quite clear that many of the sixth-year specialist schemes did not begin as fully developed, recognized programs with generally applicable specifics of admission and the

Table 1
DATE SIXTH-YEAR PROGRAM INITIATED IN LIBRARY SCHOOLS

Institution (1)	Year (2)
Atlanta	1967
Chicago	1969
Columbia	1961
Drexel[+]	1966
Emory	1966
Florida State	1967
Illinois	1964
Kent State	1968
Louisiana State[+]	1967
Maryland[+]	1967
Minnesota	1966
Peabody	1954[a]
Pittsburgh	1963
Rutgers	1966[b]
Texas	1967
Toronto	1950[c]
UCLA	1967
Wayne State	1967
Western Michigan	1966
Wisconsin	1966

[+] Program not operative, 1968-69.
a Peabody: Began 1954, suspended in 1965, reinstated in 1968.
b Rutgers: "Program really begun as such, 1967-68."
c Toronto: 6th year Master of Library Science. Toronto gives 5th year B.L.S.

like but, rather, emerged gradually from the practice of the schools of accepting qualified librarians for additional individual study. The increase in the number of such students, plus the beginning of a demand from the profession, and (usually) the availability of HEW funds seem to have been factors influencing the creation of the more formal "program" covering a year of study and resulting, generally, in a special award in the form of a certificate or degree.

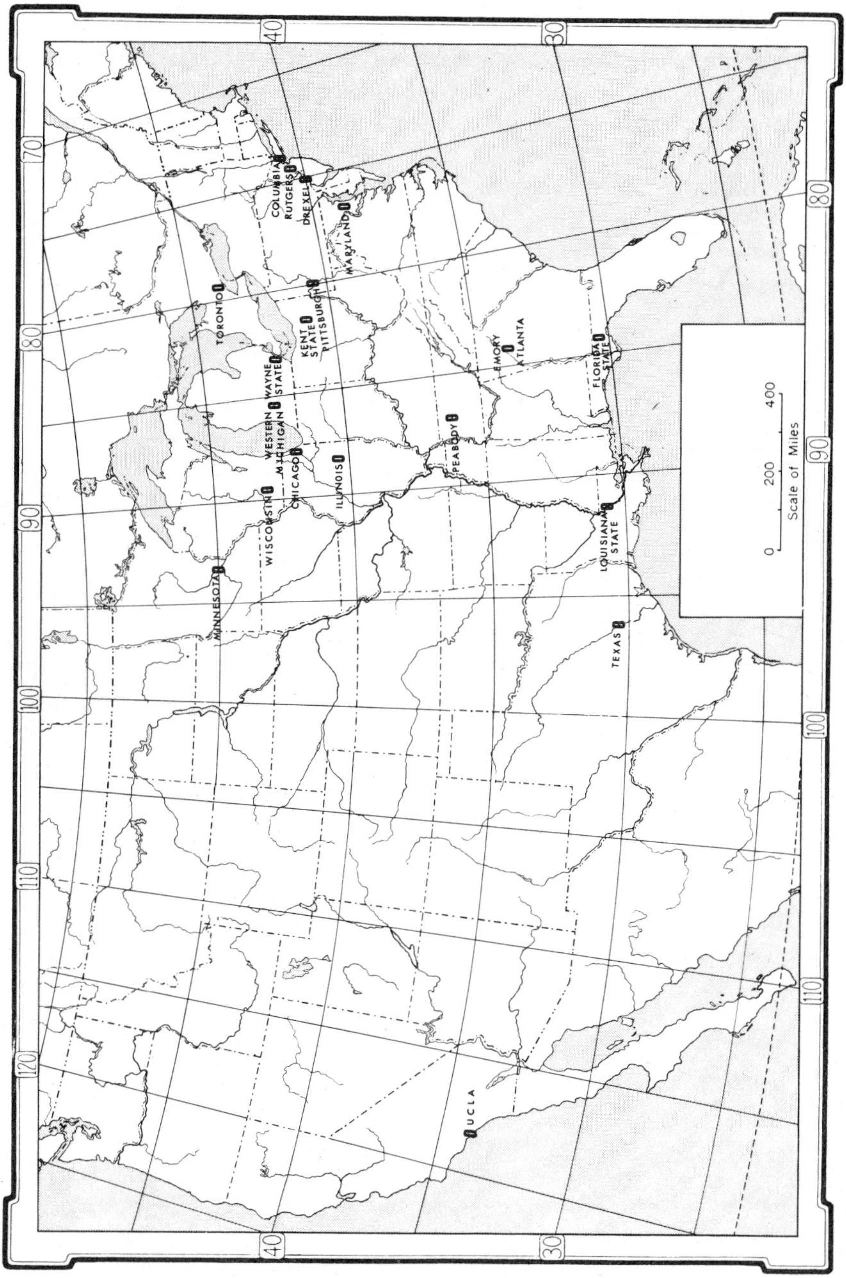

Fig. 1. Location of Sixth-Year Library Schools

Purposes and Programs

Table 2 displays the purposes of the programs as reported by the schools. There is obviously a certain amount of over-lapping of some of the purposes. Purpose A, "Specialization beyond the B.L.S/M.L.S.," for example, might be held to embrace "Special program for teaching librarianship," "Infor-

Table 2
PURPOSES OF THE SIXTH-YEAR PROGRAMS

Institution (1)	A (2)	B (3)	C (4)	D (5)	E (6)	F (7)	G (8)	H (9)
Atlanta	X	X	X					
Chicago	X							
Columbia	X	X	X	X	X	X	X	
Drexel	X	X	X	X		X		
Emory	X	X	X		X			a
Florida State	X	X	X	X	X	X	X	b
Illinois	X							
Kent State	X	X	X					
Louisiana State	X	X		X			X	
Maryland	X	X	X		X	X		
Minnesota				X				
Peabody	X			X	X	X		
Pittsburgh	X							
Rutgers	X	X	X		X	X	X	
Texas				X				
Toronto	X	X	X		X	X	X	c
UCLA	X		X			X		
Wayne State	X	X	X				X	
Western Michigan	X	X	X		X		X	d
Wisconsin	X	X	X	X	X			

A Specialization beyond the B.L.S./M.L.S.
B Update knowledge
C Upgrade professional skills
D Special program for teaching librarianship
E Preparation for administrative work in libraries
F Information science and automation skills
G Administration of instructional materials centers
H Other:

  Emory: "To meet certification requirements of State beyond master's level, i.e., Georgia has a certification level above M.A. = 95 percent of present and past students."
  Florida State: "Certification for upper ranks in library/media specialization."
  Toronto: "Training in methods of research."
  Western Michigan: "Preparation of community college librarians."

14

mation science and automation skills," "Administration of instructional materials centers," and "Preparation of community college librarians." Nonetheless, it is clear that all the schools conceive of their programs as ones which provide for at least some kind of *specialization* beyond the M.L.S.

Of particular interest, also, may be the findings that more than a third of the schools still operating programs have the teaching of librarianship as a specific specialization, and that more than a third have the area of information science and automation. The shortages of personnel in these two fields surely suggest the likelihood that these programs, at least, should find a strong acceptance among some segments of the profession. The same can probably be said of the programs of the six schools emphasizing administration of instructional materials centers, and probably of Western Michigan's program for the preparation of community college librarians.

A development which seems likely to increase general demand for some kinds of sixth-year specialist program graduates is the increasing use and recognition of a technician or technical assistant class in libraries. Employees of this kind, doing upper-level paraprofessional work, much of which has previously been done by the professional, will require supervisors. Most of the schools are including course content in the sixth-year specialized schemes which should qualify their graduates to serve in this kind of supervisory capacity.

Relation of the Sixth-Year Program to the Doctorate

As of June 1969, thirteen library schools had doctoral programs.[1] Of these, nine had sixth-year programs, as shown in table 3. Of these nine, four consider the sixth-year program "terminal," or an alternative to the doctorate; two consider it terminal *or* a first step toward the doctorate; one considers it an alternative or a first step; one considers it a first step toward the doctorate; and the ninth, Columbia, has set up the program "for those who wish to undertake advanced study without the necessity of attempting to qualify for an advanced degree," which amounts to about the same thing as

[1] Two more schools, Maryland and Syracuse, began doctoral programs in the fall of 1969.

15

Table 3
RELATIONSHIP OF THE SIXTH-YEAR PROGRAM TO THE DOCTORATE

Institution (1)	Terminal Program (2)	Alternative to Doc. (3)	First Step to Doc. (4)	No Relationship to Doc. (5)	Other (6)
Atlanta				X	
*Chicago	X		X	X	
*Columbia	X				
Drexel			X		
Emory	X				
*Florida State			X		a
*Illinois	X	X			
Kent State				X	
Louisiana State					b
*Maryland		X	X		
*Minnesota	X		X		
Peabody	X	X	X^c		
*Pittsburgh	X	X			
*Rutgers	X	X		X	
Texas				X	
Toronto				X	
UCLA	X		X		
Wayne State	X	X	X		
Western Michigan	X				
*Wisconsin	X	X			

* Offers program for doctor's degree; Maryland beginning term
   September, 1969.
a Florida: "Advanced course work."
b Louisiana: "Primarily an enrichment program."
c Peabody: "When possible."

a terminal program. The principal point here is that, with few exceptions, the schools offering doctoral programs consider their specialist programs as a separate and largely independent activity.

Of the eleven schools (of the twenty tabulated in table 3) which do not offer the doctor's degree, some consider the sixth-year program definitively terminal and some conceive of it as being either terminal, an alternative to the doctorate, or as a first step toward the doctorate.

Possible Programs at Other Schools

Fryden asks (p.243) whether other library schools will start postmaster's programs. It may be of interest to note here briefly that at least ten additional library schools are in various stages of discussion or planning for the establishment of such programs. The ten are: British Columbia, Case Western, Denver, Geneseo, Indiana, Kentucky, North Texas, Pratt, Syracuse, and Texas Woman's. The situation in these schools ranges, approximately, from Syracuse which, though not planning a program in the near future, has held tentative discussions with other departments for a dual sixth-year master's offering, to Indiana which has "definite plans to inaugurate one in the near future," and to Denver which has plans for a program to be initiated by September 1970.[2]

Admission Requirements

With one exception, the schools require the M.L.S. degree from an accredited school for admission to their sixth-year programs but four schools, while stating this as their general and normal requirement, will consider the M.L.S. from an unaccredited school and four others "might" do so. Three-quarters of the schools equate the old B.L.S. degree with the present M.L.S. and will accept students who hold it. Only one school, however, will definitely accept a student who offers undergraduate study in librarianship only, combined with a subject master's degree.

Three-quarters of the schools, again, require professional experience, ranging between one and three years, for admission. Four-fifths of the schools set no age limit, and the four which do, set it very high: one at forty years, one at forty-five, and two at fifty. Interestingly, just over a third of the schools have no grade point average (g.p.a.) requirement, presumably on the assumption that the M.L.S. degree automatically carries with it certification of a sufficiently high academic record. The schools which do set a g.p.a. admission requirement generally put it at B or 3.0/4.0, with three

[2] As of August 1970, North Texas and Denver had added sixth-year programs.

17

Table 4

ADMISSION REQUIREMENTS

Institution (1)	M.L.S. from A.L.A. Accr. School "Required" (2)	M.L.S. from Unaccr. School Also Acceptable (3)	B.L.S. Also Accept-able (4)	Undergrad. Study in L.S. with Subject M.A. (5)
Atlanta	Yes	No	No	No
Chicago	No	Yes	No	Maybe
Columbia	Yes	Yes	Yes	Maybe
Drexel	Yes	Yes	No	No
Emory	Yes	Maybe	No	No
Florida State	Yes	Maybe	Yes	No
Illinois	Yes	No	Yes[c]	No
Kent State	Yes	No	No	No
Louisiana State	Yes	d	Yes	d
Maryland	Yes	Yes	Yes	Maybe
Minnesota	Yes	No	Yes	No
Peabody	Yes	e	Yes	No
Pittsburgh	Yes	No	Yes	No
Rutgers	Yes	Maybe	Yes	Maybe
Texas	Yes	No	Yes	No
Toronto	Yes	Yes[f]	Yes	No
UCLA	Yes	No	Yes	No
Wayne State	Yes	Yes	Yes	Yes
Western Michigan	Yes	No	Yes	No
Wisconsin	Yes	Maybe	Yes	No

a   However, some students entered the program directly after the
    M.L.S. degree. See Table 7.
b   Columbia: "Satisfactory achievement on the G.R.E. will be required
    if the applicant's academic record does not provide clear and
    convincing evidence of superior scholastic achievement."
c   Illinois: "If accompanied by a master's degree in a subject field."

OR SIXTH-YEAR PROGRAMS   Table 4 (Cont.)

Professional Experience Required (6)	Age Limit (7)	Grade Point Average (8)	G.R.E. Score (9)	Foreign Language Additional to M.L.S. Requirement (10)	Other (11)
1 year[a]	No	No	No	No	References and Interviews
None	No	No	1000	No	
1 year	No	No	b	No	
2 years	No	3.0/4.0	No	No	References and Interviews
2 years	No	B	1100	No	References
2 years	50	3.5/4.0	1000	No	
2 years	No	3.75/5.00	No	No	
3 years	No	No	No	No	Interview
3 years[a]	No	3.0/4.0	No	No	
2 years	45	B	upper 50th percentile		
3 years	No	No	No	No	300 word essay
2 years[a]	No	2.0/3.0	900	No	References
None	No	3.0/4.0	No	No	
None	No	No	No	No	Interview
1-2 years[a]	40	B	1200	No	References
None	No	B	No		Interview
None	No	3.0/4.0	1200	No	
2 years	50's	B+	No	No	Interviews
1 year	No	2.25/4.0	"acceptable score"	No	
2 years	No	No	No	No	Statement of Goals

d   Louisiana: "Must have M.L.S. or B.L.S. from A.L.A. accredited school or master's degree in another field or a minimum of 18 hours acceptable credit hours in librarianship."

e   Peabody: "In special cases."

f   Toronto: "A B.L.S. or M.L.S. from an unaccredited school is acceptable with make-up courses."

19

schools having a somewhat higher requirement than this. About half of the schools have a Graduate Record Examination (G.R.E.) requirement and set the acceptable combined score between 900 and 1200. No foreign language other than that required for the M.L.S. degree is called for, and aside from references and interviews, which are required by half of the schools, no other special stipulations for the sixth-year programs are indicated.

These data are shown in detail in table 4, and the situation may be summed up approximately as follows: for admission to their sixth-year programs the schools require graduation from an ALA accredited school, some professional experience (five exceptions), no age limit (four exceptions), a B or better g.p.a. (seven exceptions), no foreign language additional to that called for by the M.L.S. degree; about half of the schools require what they deem to be a satisfactory score on the G.R.E. None of this seems surprising except, perhaps, for the relative inattention to the prognostic or additional evaluative potential of the G.R.E., and no special additional comment appears called for. The fact seems to be that the schools have generally set satisfactorily high admission requirements for their sixth-year programs.

That the schools are adhering closely to their stated admission requirements, at least with respect to the prior degree held by those who have completed the programs, is evidenced by the data in table 5. As reported by the schools, a total of at least 178 of the graduates had either the M.L.S., the old B.L.S., or the Toronto B.L.S. (Not all schools were able to report data for all graduates.) The twenty-three subject master's degrees shown in table 5 are almost all additional to, rather than "substitutes" for, the B.L.S. or M.L.S. Whether this figure of twenty-three is considered "high" or "low" is a value judgment which the reader will have to make for himself. It seems to the writer that the percentage of approximately 13 is probably about as high as one could expect and, on the whole, not a bad showing, although it is safe to say that the profession would welcome—and many, if not most, library positions would benefit from—more persons with advanced subject education.

The schools are also closely adhering, at least de facto, to the requirement, which most set, that applicants for the

Table 5
KINDS OF DEGREES HELD BY GRADUATES OF SIXTH-YEAR PROGRAMS
(FOURTEEN SCHOOLS)

Institution (1)	5th-Year B.L.S. Male (2)	5th-Year B.L.S. Female	M.L.S. Male (3)	M.L.S. Female	Subject M.A. Male (4)	Subject M.A. Female	Other Male (5)	Other Female
Columbia								
Emory				7				
Florida State			1	9				
Illinois	1		7	8				
Louisiana State		4	5	7	6	4		
Maryland		1	2	2				
Minnesota				1				
Peabody		4	2	3				
Pittsburgh		1	17	26	4	2		
Texas				5				
Toronto	10	37	1	0	3	2	3[a]	1[a]
UCLA				3		1		
Western Michigan		2	1					
Wisconsin		4	2	1	1			
Total	11	53	38	72	14	9	3	1

a Toronto, Male 1 S. African, 2 Indian Diplomas in Librarianship;
Female 1 British, F.L.A.

Table 6
YEARS OF PROFESSIONAL EXPERIENCE OF ENROLLED STUDENTS
BEFORE THE PROGRAM
N = 131

Institution (1)	1 (2)	2 (3)	3 (4)	4 (5)	5-7 (6)	8-9 (7)	10-12 (8)	More than 12 (9)
Columbia		1			1	1		5
Emory					1		3	3
Florida State		2	1		1	1		4
Illinois			1		5	4	1	3
Louisiana State				4	3	1	2	5
Maryland			1		2		1	1
Minnesota								1
Peabody					1		2	1
Pittsburgh	3	2	1	2	4	4	1	6
Texas		1		1	1			
Toronto	3	2	2	2	5	7	4	8
UCLA								
Western Michigan								2
Wisconsin	1				1		1	4
Total	7	8	10	5	25	18	15	43

sixth-year program have had professional experience after the
B.L.S./M.L.S. Table 6, which also refers to graduates, shows
the data on this point. However, as shown in table 7, four
schools—Atlanta, Louisiana State, Peabody, and Texas—
which set a requirement of experience, have admitted some
students without it. It is the writer's viewpoint that at least a

Table 7
NUMBER OF STUDENTS ENTERING SIXTH-YEAR PROGRAM IMMEDIATELY
AFTER B.L.S./M.L.S. DEGREE

Institution (1)	No. From This Library School (2)	No. From Another Library School (3)
Atlanta	7	1
Chicago	n.a.	n.a.
Columbia	0	0
Drexel	0	0
Emory	0	0
Florida State	0	0
Illinois	0	0
Kent State	0	0
Louisiana State	2	2
Maryland	0	0
Minnesota	0	0
Peabody	3	2
Pittsburgh	19	0
Rutgers	data not available	
Texas	5	2
Toronto	3	2
UCLA	5	1
Wayne State	0	0
Western Michigan	0	0
Wisconsin	0	0
Total	44	10

year or two of professional experience is desirable as a pre-requisite for the kind of program under consideration, chiefly on the grounds that experience is likely to show the librarian what he is most interested in and best capable of doing and, at the same time, provide him with some practice and maturity which will enable him to profit more from further study. It is recognized, however, that the contrary view is held by many; certainly it is held by the administration and faculty of the five schools that do not set professional experience as an admission requirement (see table 4).

Curricula

In view of the numerous different specializations offered by the several schools, the data on this topic are exceedingly varied and, for the most part, impossible to generalize upon. Nine, or almost half of the schools, require (required) no single course or seminar of all students. Seven of the schools, a little over a third, require (required) a course or seminar in some topic such as "Research in Librarianship," "Directed Independent Study," or "Methods of Research." And seven, again, have one or more specific course or seminar requirements which depend upon the student's field of specialization, for example, Library Education and Supervised Teaching, for those in a program for library school teaching; or Introduction to Information Retrieval, and Library Mechanization, for the student in an information science specialization program. With respect to curricula, therefore, the schools appear to have set up course programs which are, first, highly flexible, and, second, in large part if not almost wholly, individually tailored to the needs of the student and the particular specialization upon which he has entered.

Of the sixteen schools which had programs in the spring of 1969, and had had them for a year or more, ten had developed new courses for existing and new fields of specialization, and two other schools had instituted new courses, though not exclusively or specifically for the sixth-year program. As in the case of curricula in general, the new courses of the ten schools vary greatly in line with the purposes and specializations of the schools. The following examples may be of interest as indicating some of the kinds of instruction now available for sixth-year students: Studies in Reading; Library Curriculum Materials; School Librarianship; Supervision of School Media Services; Rare Books; Information Science; Theological Library Administration; Curriculum Materials; Advanced Administration of School Libraries; Programming Theory for Information Handling; Education for Librarianship; Automation and Data Processing; Systems Analysis; Documentation Theory; Data Processing for Information Retrieval; The Community College; Public Library Administration; Modern Archives Administration; Current Issues in Work with Children; Public Library Systems; Literature of the Social Sciences; Literature of the Humanities; Comparative Librarianship; and Problems in Library Education.

A number of these courses are available in two or more schools. Taken together, they represent a very substantial enrichment of the schools' curricula and, to some extent at least, a probable upgrading of instructional content in some areas. Both of these desirable developments are the direct result of the establishment of the sixth-year specialist programs.

Further, at least half a dozen of the schools plan additional course or fields-of-specialization development in the next two to five years. Among the courses and/or fields contemplated are: School Library Supervision; Library Education; Administration; American Library Studies; Medical Librarianship; Law Librarianship; Information Science; Archives and Oral History; Junior College Library Administration; and Urban Librarianship. Again, several of these apply to two or more schools.

Course Work outside the Library School

Although few schools formally require their students to take courses in other disciplines, such course work is universally encouraged and, when taken, counted toward completion of the sixth-year-program unit requirement. The number of units which may be taken varies, as might be expected, with the specific needs of the individual student but is likely to have a maximum limit approximating half of the total program. The nature of the work taken in other

24

departments is almost infinitely varied and may be anything from legal bibliography to statistics to Latin-American culture to child psychology. It would appear, then, that the schools are paying substantial attention to the contribution which other disciplines can make to the preparation of their students and are exercising great flexibility in this regard. The attention and the flexibility are, understandably, greater than is the case with most programs for the M.L.S. Some details, by schools, for the sixth-year programs are given in table 8.

Table 8
COURSES TAKEN BY SIXTH-YEAR STUDENTS IN OTHER SUBJECTS OR DEPARTMENTS

Institution (1)	Outside Courses Counted in Required Units (2)	Number of Units Which May be Taken Outside Lib. Sch. (3)	Outside Course Work Encouraged (4)	Outside Courses Required (5)	Number of Outside Units Required (6)
Atlanta	Yes	18 s.h.	Yes	Yes	18 s.h.
Chicago	Yes				
Columbia	Yes	varies	Yes	No	
Drexel	Yes	21 q.h.	Yes	No	
Emory	Yes	Indiv. needs	Yes	No	
Florida State	Yes	No specific no.	Yes		
Illinois	Yes	4 s.h.	Yes	No	
Kent State	Yes	varies	Yes	No	
Louisiana State	Yes	varied	Yes	No	
Maryland	Yes	varied	Yes	No	
Minnesota	Yes	24 q.h.max.	Yes	Yes	6 q.h.
Peabody	Yes	9-15 s.h.	Yes	No	
Pittsburgh	Yes	12 s.h.max.	Yes	No	
Rutgers	Yes	varies	Yes	No	
Texas	Yes	varies	Yes	No	
Toronto	Yes	Half	Yes	No	
UCLA	Yes	varies	Yes	Yes	varies
Wayne State	Yes	15 q.h.	Yes	Yes	15 q.h.
Western Michigan	Yes	9-12 s.h.	Yes		
Wisconsin	Yes	Half	Yes		6 s.h.

s.h. = semester hours   q.h. = quarter hours

25

Enrollment

Table 9 and figure 2 show enrollment and enrollment trends in total number of students, 1960 - 61 to 1968 - 69. Omitted are the 1950 - 60 data for Toronto, a somewhat special case which, in that period, had 87 enrollees. Two facts are immediately apparent: first, the almost steady and overall very great enrollment increase from 1960 - 61 through 1967 - 68; and, second, the drop in enrollment from that year to 1968 - 69. The first fact seems to augur well, or would have seemed to augur well, for the acceptability and viability of the programs were it not for the second fact. If it were to be assumed that the three schools—Drexel, Louisiana State, and Maryland—which did not continue their programs in 1968 - 69 would have had enrollments in that year comparable to their enrollments in 1967 - 68, there would have been an additional 23 enrollees in 1968 - 69. This would then have increased the actual 1968 - 69 enrollment from 216 to 239.

It is also possible that the decrease in Title II-B fellowships from 58 in 1967 - 68 to 47 in 1968 - 69 may have had an adverse effect on enrollment in the latter year. However, even adding the difference of 11 to 239 gives a total "potential" 1968 - 69 enrollment of only 250, or 15 fewer than the actual enrollment in 1967 - 68. Inquiry did not reveal whether the decrease might be meaningful in the sense that it was the beginning of a possible trend, or whether, on the other hand, it was a phenomenon of a single year, due to chance and unknown causes and wholly lacking in long-range significance. It seems, however, worthwhile to suggest that the eight schools which have experienced enrollment decreases in 1968 - 69 should closely watch their enrollments in future years and, if they continue to decline, attempt to determine the causes.

It is interesting to observe from table 9 that enrollment through 1967 - 68 was composed of 223 males and 442 females, a ratio of almost exactly 1:2. Similarly, from table 10, the 196 graduates through 1968 consisted of 56 males and 140 females, or a ratio of 1:2.5. Both ratios reveal, of course, a substantially higher proportion of males than that which obtains in the profession at large on the North American continent. The reasons for the difference are probably

Table 9

ENROLLMENT IN THE SIXTH-YEAR PROGRAMS*

Institution (1)	1960-61 M (2)	F	1961-62 M (3)	F	1962-63 M (4)	F	1963-64 M (5)	F	1964-65 M (6)	F	1965-66 M (7)	F	1966-67 M (8)	F	1967-68 M (9)	F	1968-69 Year Total (10)	F.T.E.a (10)	Grand Total Enrollment (11)
Atlanta													2	4	2	10	9		27
Chicago																	6	[6]	6
Columbia											1		1	1	2	6	5	[5.5]	20
Drexel													8	6	8		2^b		24
Emory												6		9		10	1		26
Florida State															1	9	11	[11]	21
Illinois							6^c	4^c	4^c	5^c	5	6	9^c	6^c	6	5	18	[14.6]	74
Kent State																	1	[1]	1
Louisiana State													2	8	5	5			20
Maryland															2	3			5
Minnesota													1	4	2	2	1	[1]	10
Peabody	2^d	2^d	1^d	6^d	1^d	7^d	1^d	7^d	1^d	6^d					1	4	5	[3]	44
Pittsburgh											5		16	15	36	34	56	[30]	167
Rutgers															1	3	14		18
Texas															5		2		7
Toronto^e	3	2	6	9	4	6	10	19	16	22	20	55	15	43	22	54	57	[36]	339
UCLA														1	1	1	3	[2.3]	6
Wayne State															1	1	5		7
Western Michigan											1		3	9	5	10	15	[6.6]	43
Wisconsin													1	3	2	5	5	[5]	16
Total by Year and Sex	5	4	7	15	5	12	18	31	22	39	20	55	58	108	88	177	216		881
Total Enrollment by Year	9		22		18		49		61		75		166		265		216		

* Fall, and summer when discrete and applicable.

a F.T.E. figures given when available.

b Drexel: Program discontinued spring 1968; however, students already enrolled were allowed to continue.

c Illinois: Data given as: summer 1964, 4 total; summer 1965, 8 total; summer 1967, 8 total; arbitrarily divided

half and half and added to fall figures in this table.

d Peabody: Data given as: 1960-61, 4 total; 1961-62, 7 total; 1962-63, 8 total; 1963-64, 8 total; 1964-65, 7 total; arbitrarily divided in above ratio on questionnaire internal evidence.

e Toronto: 1950-60 inclusive: 21 males and 69 females enrolled.

27

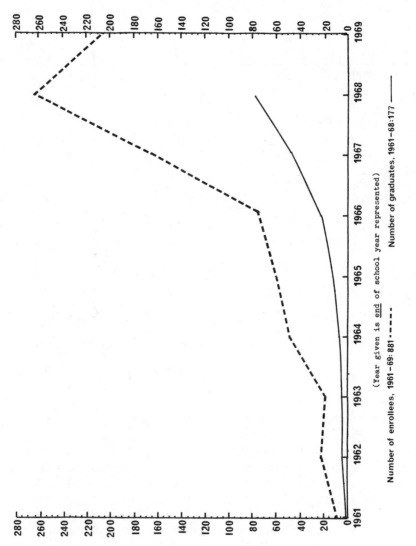

(Year given is <u>end</u> of school year represented)

Number of enrollees, 1961–69: 881 ------   Number of graduates, 1961–68:177 ——————

Fig. 2. Enrollment and Graduate Trends

Table 10

NUMBER OF STUDENTS WHO HAVE COMPLETED SIXTH-YEAR PROGRAMS

Institution (1)	1961 (2) M	F	1962 (3) M	F	1963 (4) M	F	1964 (5) M	F	1965 (6) M	F	1966 (7) M	F	1967 (8) M	F	1968 (9) M	F	Total (10)
Columbia										4		1	1	1	2	6	15
Emory											6	1					7
Florida State															1	9	10
Illinois					1				1			4	3	2	3	1	15
Louisiana State													2	8	5	5	20
Maryland															2	3	5
Minnesota														1			1
Peabody	2			3	1		1		1		1						9
Pittsburgh							1	1	1	2		5	7	8	8	11	44
Texas																5	5
Toronto a			1		1	1	4	2	2	3	2	1	1	9	2	5	52 a
UCLA																3	3
Western Michigan														1	1	1	3
Wisconsin													1	2	1	3	7
Total for year by sex	2		1	3	2	2	1	6	3	10	3	19	15	33	25	52	196 a
Total by year	2		4		4		7		13		22		48		77		

a Toronto: Includes 1950-60 inclusive; 4 males and 15 females
   completed the program.

clear to those familiar with library education and the library profession in America, but may be briefly stated here.

Of the female majority which has traditionally turned to the library profession, many are young women who, after a few years' employment, leave it for marriage, and consequently have no interest in further study. They are automatically eliminated as potential candidates for a sixth-year program. It may be assumed, also, that an additional group of female librarians anticipate marriage in the future, rather than a lifelong professional career, and therefore have little or no interest in advanced education. On the other hand, a male librarian normally expects to remain one all his life, and a

29

majority have, or anticipate having, a family to support. Consequently, the male librarian is, in general, more interested than the female in advanced study which will probably lead to higher position and better salary. Without the slightest pejorative implication for the distaff side, it is unquestionably to the benefit of the profession that a higher than normal proportion of males is entering and graduating from the sixth-year programs.

From the point of view of service to the profession, the number of students who have completed the programs—and, as noted hereafter, generally received some kind of certificate or diploma in recognition of that fact—is no doubt of greater interest and significance than the number of enrollees just discussed. Many of the latter, dropping out of school after a brief attendance and/or after taking as few as one or two courses, have presumably not greatly benefited either themselves or the libraries in which they were subsequently employed. The data on graduates are shown in table 10. The yearly increases, especially beginning in 1965, are steady and substantial. From 1965 to 1966 the number of graduates increased by nearly 70 percent; from 1966 to 1967 the increase was nearly 120 percent; and from 1967 to 1968 it was 60 percent.

As already mentioned, the fourteen schools, which by the end of 1968 had produced graduates, had graduated a total of 196—a mean of 14. However, the 52 graduates of Toronto and the 44 of Pittsburgh represent almost 50 percent of the total, whereas nine schools graduated 10 or fewer, and seven schools graduated 7 or fewer. All these seven schools, however, began their programs in 1966 or later. It will be exceedingly interesting to observe, in future years, the figures on graduates, both by individual schools and as a total. Indeed, it is perhaps not going too far to suggest that these figures will say much concerning the acceptance of the concept by prospective students and by the profession as a whole, and therefore provide a strong indicator of the probable viability of the programs. The data at hand appear to indicate increased acceptance and, therefore, the very strong likelihood of viability.

The student attrition rate seems very high. If we subtract from the total reported enrollment of 881 (table 9) the 216 enrollees of 1968 - 69, and one-quarter of the 1967 - 68 enrollment of 265—students who may have started part time in that year—the result is 601. The 196 students who have graduated through 1967 - 68 represent fewer than one-third of the maximum possible graduates. Or, put differently, 405 "enrollees" never completed the program—a figure more than twice as large as the number who did. It should be remembered here that "enrollees" is not quite the same as separate individuals, since some students extend their studies over two or more years and are therefore counted twice or more as enrollees. The extent of the difference is indeterminate, but even if it is as high as 25 percent, the attrition is still great. Whether the schools can do anything about this high loss in time and effort—and the loss to the profession—is a question only they can determine, but it would appear desirable that they attempt to reduce the attrition rate at least by making as certain as possible that more of the students admitted are capable of completing the programs, and prepared and committed to do so.

Graduation Requirements

The data on this topic are shown in table 11, reveal no surprises, call for little comment, and may be briefly summarized. Without exception, the sixth-year specialist programs call for at least a full year of study, with four schools requiring a year plus a summer session. (The number of quarter or semester units necessary to complete the program is not given in the table simply because these units correspond, in every case, to at least a full year of study.) All but three of the schools have a minimum residence requirement, but this requirement varies from a semester to two semesters, or its equivalent—three quarters. The g.p.a. is, for four-fifths of the schools, a B; for two schools it is slightly higher than this, and for one it is slightly lower.

Fewer than half of the schools require a thesis or a research project. Fryden (p.238), speaking to the thesis or research-project requirement, raises this question:

> At this point one begins to ask where library students acquire practice in carrying out extended pieces of

research. To the extent that these people will eventually work toward doctorates, where will they have obtained experience which will be useful in planning and writing the doctoral dissertation?

The question seems a fair one and, as Fryden immediately afterward notes, it is not at all theoretical. Despite the fact that a majority of the doctoral library schools conceive of the sixth-year specialist programs as in some sense terminal, 40 percent of all graduates consider the sixth-year program as a possible first step toward the doctorate, and a considerable number of the graduates do, immediately or later, enter upon doctoral study. Twenty-six graduates were doctoral students in spring 1969. The question seems not entirely unfair, also,

Table 11
REQUIREMENTS THE STUDENTS MUST MEET TO COMPLETE THE PROGRAM SUCCESSFULLY

Institution (1)	Duration of Program (2)	Residence Requirement (3)	G.P.A. to be Maintained (4)	Thesis or Research Project (5)	Comprehensive Exam (6)	Other (7)
Atlanta	1 acad.yr.	1 acad.yr.	B	Yes	No	Nat.Teacher's Exam T-5 Cert. Georgia
Chicago	"	3 quart.	C+	No	Yes	
Columbia	"	2 sem.	B	No	No	
Drexel	"	None	$\frac{3.0}{4.0}$	Yes	No	
Emory	"	3 quart. 1 qu.full time	$\frac{3.3}{4.0}$	No	No	
Florida State	"	3 quart.	B	No	No	
Illinois	"	1 acad.yr.	B	No	No	
Kent State	"	3 quart.	$\frac{3.0}{4.0}$	No	No	
Louisiana State	"	2 sem.	$\frac{3.0}{4.0}$	Yes	No	
Maryland	"	2 sem.		No	No	
Minnesota	1 acad.yr. + Summ.Sess.	30 credits	$\frac{3.0}{4.0}$	Yes	No	
Peabody	"	1 sem.	$\frac{2.0}{4.0}$	Yes	No	
Pittsburgh	1 acad.yr.	2 trimesters	B	No	No	
Rutgers	"	None	B	No	No	
Texas	1 acad.yr. + Summ.Sess.	1 year	B	No	No	Practice Teaching
Toronto	1 acad.yr.	None	B	optional	No	1 Foreign Lang.
UCLA	"	3-4 quarters	$\frac{3.0}{4.0}$	Yes	No	Internship in some fields of specialization
Wayne State	1 acad.yr. + Summ.Sess.	33 units	$\frac{3.0}{4.0}$	Yes	No	
Western Michigan	1 cal.yr.	1 sem.	$\frac{3.25}{4.0}$	Yes	Yes	
Wisconsin	1 acad.yr.	1 sem.	$\frac{3.0}{4.0}$	Yes	Yes	

with respect to the graduates—more than a fifth of the total— who are teaching in library schools. Some of these graduates are in the doctoral schools and have responsibility for doctoral students. It is hard to see how they can adequately discharge this responsibility if they have had no personal experience in the planning and prosecution of a research project. It might even be argued that the graduates teaching in nondoctoral schools would profit in their teaching, and in their evaluation of professional literature, from this experience.

There is a further, related consideration. We shall not, in the foreseeable future, have a sufficient number of doctoral graduates to meet the demand. Consequently, whatever the library schools can do to attract and encourage good doctoral students represents a major contribution to the profession. In librarianship, as in other disciplines, one of the most useful means for determining if the student has the potential for successful doctoral work is his performance as a neophyte researcher. This involves, chiefly, the critique of published research on the one hand, and the selection,. definition, planning, organization, and prosecution of a small piece of research of his own, on the other. It therefore follows that the more sixth-year program students who can be exposed to, and judged by, this kind of activity, the greater the benefit to the profession.

Budgetary Support

Only four of the schools received additional funds for faculty, only two for other staff, only five for library materials, only three for other facilities. At first glance, this might seem to be a highly questionable state of affairs and imply inadequate provision for, and concern about, the programs. However, two related facts suggest the likelihood that neither implication is, in fact, warranted. In the first place, as already shown in table 9, enrollment figures, except at Pittsburgh and Toronto, have always been small—so small, in fact, that the sixth-year program enrollees could readily be absorbed in the total student body and by existing faculty. At the same time—as numerous schools made clear—general student

enrollment increases were already producing additional
faculty F.T.E. (full-time equivalent) and other kinds of support, some of which could be, and have been, used on behalf
of the sixth-year programs. Despite the addition of new
courses, therefore, faculty load has not increased. It seems
reasonable to believe, then, that the schools for the present
do not need more additional support than they are normally
securing, and will not, until the number of sixth-year program students increases considerably. Table 12 provides detailed information on this topic.

Table 12
EXTRA BUDGETARY PROVISIONS MADE FOR INITIATION OF
SIXTH-YEAR PROGRAMS

Institution (1)	Faculty (2)	Other Staff (3)	Library Materials (4)	Equipment (5)	Extra Facilities (6)
Atlanta	No	No	Yes	Yes	No
Chicago	No	No	No	No	No
Columbia	No	No	No	No	No
Drexel	No	No	No	No	No
Emory	No	No	No	No	No
Florida State	No	No	No	No	No
Illinois	No	No	No	No	No
Kent State	No	No	No	No	No
Louisiana State	Yes	Yes	Yes	Yes	No
Maryland	No	No	No	No	No
Minnesota	No	No	No	No	No
Peabody	Yes	No	No	No	
Pittsburgh	No	No	No	No	No
Rutgers	No	No	No	No	No
Texas	No	No	No	No	No
Toronto	No[1]	No[1]	Yes	No	No
UCLA	No	No	No	No	No
Wayne State	No	No	No	No	No
Western Michigan	Yes	No	Yes	Yes	No
Wisconsin	Yes	Yes	Yes	No	No

1 Toronto: No initial budgetary provision, but since 1964, extra
provision made for Faculty and other Staff.

More than three-quarters of the U.S. schools have received support from HEW. For a majority of the schools, probably at least two-thirds, the importance of this support has been determinant, and perhaps crucial, for the programs. Several schools have indicated that planning and implementation of the programs could hardly have been accomplished without the federal aid and, additionally, that it had a positive psychological effect upon higher authority on the campuses. At some schools more, and more substantial, HEW fellowships were available than there were at the disposal of all departments in the humanities. The forty to sixty grants available annually have been a not insignificant factor in recruiting and enrollment. All the schools had scholarship aid, most of it from this source. Fryden, in fact (p.242), asks whether the programs may be wholly dependent for their continuance on federal funds. The answer is no. While a few schools admit that the cutting off of, or a drastic reduction in, government aid would seriously handicap their efforts and would probably reduce the level of their operations, none believes that its program would cease. There is, therefore, a strong institutional commitment to the sixth-year activity.

Certificates, Diplomas, and Degrees

As shown in table 13, all but four of the twenty schools which offer, or have offered, sixth-year programs award (ed) for their successful completion either a certificate or a degree—thirteen certificates and four degrees, one school having both. In half the schools the award is made by the university itself, in three cases by the library school, in two cases by the graduate school. As shown in column 4 of the table, there is a much more, indeed, a very wide variation in the title of the award. There are, in fact, almost as many different designations as there are awards—fourteen in all. This seems a distinctly disadvantageous situation. Who, even in the library profession, is likely to be aware of all these different titles and to recognize that, despite their varied phraseology, they represent the same amount and frequently the same kind of advanced professional education? Certainly, boards of library trustees, civil service agencies, institutional

Table 13
CERTIFICATE OR DEGREE AWARDED FOR SUCCESSFUL COMPLETION
OF SIXTH-YEAR PROGRAMS

Institution (1)	Certif-icate (2)	Degree (3)	Title of Award (4)	By Whom Awarded (5)
Atlanta	Yes		T-6 Cert. in Lib. Service	Georgia St. Dept.of Educ.
Chicago	Yes		Cert. of Advanced Study	Library School
Columbia	No			
Drexel	Yes		Advanced Cert. in Lib. Sci.	University
Emory	Yes		Dipl. for Advanced Study in Librarianship	Graduate School
Florida State	Yes	Yes	Cert.for Post-Master's Progr. Adv. Master's Degree	Library School University
Illinois	Yes		Cert. of Advanced Study	University
Kent State	Yes		Cert. of Advanced Study in Lib. Science	University
Louisiana State	No			
Maryland	Yes		Certificate of Completion	Library School
Minnesota	Yes		Sp.Cert.in Lib.Sci.Teaching	University
Peabody		Yes	Specialist in Education	University
Pittsburgh	Yes		Advanced Certificate	University
Rutgers	No			
Texas	No			
Toronto		Yes	Master of Library Science	University
UCLA	Yes		Cert. of Specialization in Library Science	University
Wayne State	Yes		Education Specialist Cert.	College of Education
Western Michigan		Yes	Specialist in Education	University
Wisconsin*	Yes		Specialist in Librarianship	Graduate School

* Wisconsin: People with B.L.S. who satisfy M.L.S. requirements and
  obtain specialist certificate also receive M.L.S. degree.

personnel officers, city managers, school boards, and others concerned with the employment of librarians cannot possibly be expected to comprehend this multiplicity. It would seem highly desirable that the Association of American Library Schools and, perhaps, the C.O.A. attempt to secure agreement among the accredited schools on a single certificate title or, at most, upon not more than two or three titles.

It would also seem desirable that the schools which give no award do so. It is clearly some employment advantage for a person to be able to say, "I received the Diploma in Advanced Study from the _____ Library School," rather

than, simply, "I had a year of advanced study at _____."
Further, an award, that is, a handle to a program, is more
likely to be granted a recognized position classification in the
pay plan than is an undescribed year of study. The
students/graduates with whom this point was discussed were
unanimously in agreement.

In recent years there has been considerable talk in the profession at, least in its educational branch, of the probable
desirability of changing the present fifth-year M.L.S. to a
sixth-year M.L.S., that is, to make the basic, minimum education standard for entrance into the profession two years of
postbaccalaureate professional study.[3] Very few members of
library school faculties today feel that a good job of preparing the prospective librarian can really be done within the
space of a single year. Librarianship has broadened and
deepened greatly since the end of World War II and has taken
unto itself whole new, complex, and important areas, such as
information science and retrieval. There is just too much subject matter for adequate coverage in a year. If accredited
library schools should move toward a two-year master's
degree, most of those which have sixth-year specialist plans
would be in a favorable position for making the conversion.

As a concluding note to this chapter, it is of interest to
observe that specialist programs at the level with which this
study is concerned now exist in numerous fields and that, as
in the case of librarianship, they are a recent innovation:

> Studies have indicated that acceptance of the
> [Specialist] degree is growing; the number of
> institutions using some form of the Specialist degree has
> grown rapidly in the last decade.
>
> The Specialist degree program has been accepted by
> many states as the minimum for preparing educational
> administrators, supervisors and consultants, social
> welfare workers, conservationists, public health per-
> sonnel, psychometrists, guidance personnel and other
> professional personnel. . . .

[3] See, e.g., University of California, Los Angeles, School of Library
Service, "Third Departmental Conference on Courses and Programs, 26
March 1970," Departmental Announcements and Memoranda, 70 - 81,
21 April 1970.

Specialist degree programs are intended for those preparing for positions which call for a higher level of study than the Master's degree but not the emphasis on research required for the Doctor's degree.

A major object of such programs is to strengthen an individual's area of specialization. . . . Specialist degree programs are functionally oriented toward the student's professional objectives.

The Specialist degree is not a research degree but the student should become well acquainted with research in his field of specialization and, to a lesser extent, in related or cognate fields. *He must also be guaranteed adequate opportunities for obtaining the necessary background in research methodology.* [Italics added.] [4]

The foregoing quotation is perhaps enough to demonstrate that the sixth-year specialist programs in the library field closely parallel what is being done in numerous other professional fields.

[4] American Association of State Colleges and Universities, National Conference on the Intermediate Degree, *The Specialist Degree* (Washington, D.C.: American Assn. of State Colleges and Universities, 1969 [?]), p.1 - 3.

| Chapter 4 | # The Graduates |

This chapter presents certain characteristics of those who have graduated from the sixth-year specialist programs. The reader may also wish to consult table 5, page 21, for the preprogram degrees held by the graduates, and table 6, page 21, for the extent of their prior professional experience.

Number and Distribution by School

As noted in chapter 3, the twenty schools which have, or have had, sixth-year specialist programs report a total of 196 graduates through 1967 - 68. The figure is, however, grossly misleading: six schools—Atlanta, Chicago, Drexel, Kent State, Rutgers, and Wayne State—had no graduates, either because of the recency of establishment of the program or because it was in existence too short a time; and two schools—Pittsburgh with 44 graduates, and Toronto with 52—account for nearly half of the total. Of the remaining twelve schools, two had 7 graduates, two had 5, two had 3, and one had 1. In other words, seven of the twelve schools had 7 or fewer graduates. These twelve schools graduated a total of 100 students, the mean and median being, respectively, 8.3 and 7. If Pittsburgh's 44 and Toronto's 52 are included, making the total of 196, the mean and median for the fourteen schools are 14 and 8. Quite clearly, most of the programs have not yet produced a large number of graduates, a fact which is certainly explained, not only by the recency of the programs, but also by the related fact that the profession as a whole is not fully aware of them and has not established official position classifications and salary schedules for them.

A questionnaire (Appendix C) was sent to the 191 graduates for whom effective addresses were available. Returns were received from 157, a response of 82.2 percent. Of these, 153, or 80 percent, of the total deliverable (78 percent of all graduates) were usable. The maximum N for the tables in this chapter is therefore 153, except in the case of table 20 which is based upon data supplied by the schools. However, not all graduates responded to all questions in the questionnaire, and 26 graduates are now doctoral students; as a consequence, N is less than 153 for most tables. The N for each table is noted under the table head. The data, by schools, for graduates and questionnaire responses are shown in table 14. This table, like all others in this chapter, covers only the fourteen schools which have had graduates.

Table 14
GRADUATES AND QUESTIONNAIRES (FOURTEEN SCHOOLS)

Institution (1)	No. of Graduates Reported (2)	No. of Deliverable Questionnaires (3)	No. of Questionnaires Returned (4)	Percentage of Questionnaires Returned Column 4 ÷ 3 (5)	No. of Questionnaires Received Too Late (6)	No. of Questionnaires Otherwise Unusable (7)	No. of Usable Questionnaires column 4−[(6)+(7)] (8)	Percentage of Usable Questionnaires column 8 ÷ 2 (9)
Columbia	15	13	10	76	2		8	53
Emory	7	7	7	100			7	100
Florida State	10	10	9	90			9	90
Illinois	15	15	14	93			14	93
Louisiana State	20	19	18	94			18	90
Maryland	5	5	5	100			5	100
Minnesota	1	1	1	100			1	100
Peabody	9	9	5	55			5	55
Pittsburgh	44	43	32	74			32	72
Texas	5	5	5	100			5	100
Toronto	52	51	39	76		2	37	71
UCLA	3	3	3	100			3	100
Western Michigan	3	3	2	66			2	66
Wisconsin	7	7	7	100			7	100
Total	196	191	157	82.2	2	2	153	78

At this point it is necessary to speak to the question of the nonrespondent—a point that is almost always ignored in library literature. Statistically, the nonrespondent represents a potential hazard, since the reasons for his nonresponse may relate to facts which, were he a respondent, would significantly alter conclusions and generalizations based solely on data from those who did respond. Consider, for example, in the present situation, the question of salaries currently received by graduates. The highest salaries are probably ones received by those in more important positions and/or in larger institutions. These people *may* feel themselves too busy to respond; they *may* be persons who, because of position, are flooded with questionnaires and will not take the time to answer another. If so, the responses received will tend to be from those with the lower salaries and will not reflect, in proper proportion, those with the higher ones. Consequently, a mean figure, for example, would be lower than it actually should be. Quite the opposite result would occur if those with the lowest salaries did not respond or, responding, failed to state their salaries, because they deemed them too low; that is, they were, in effect, ashamed to report how little they were receiving.

A major consideration in the potential hazard of the non-respondent is the proportion of returns received. Here it is unusually high—82.2 percent of the total population. The higher the proportion, the less likelihood that data from the nonrespondents would affect the results. That is, if the total population were 100, and data were received from 99, the statistical chances of the 1 nonrespondent affecting the results would be exceedingly low. Further, unless this 1 were a very exceptional case, he would affect most measures, such as mean and range, very little or not at all.

The measure commonly used in an attempt to obviate the hazard of the nonrespondent is to try to persuade a random sample of nonrespondents to provide at least certain key data, to assume that these nonrespondents are representative of all, and then to compare their responses with replies already received to see if there are statistically significant differences. Inasmuch as two follow-ups to nonrespondents were used in the present study, this device is not practicable, and resort must be made to other kinds of evidence.

One such is comparisons between kinds and levels of positions held by respondents and nonrespondents. Of the 43 nonrespondent, nondeliverable group, 11 were doctoral students, and for another 18 no employment data were available. The kinds and levels of position of the remaining 14 are wholly unexceptional and indistinguishable from those of the respondents. Similarly, a comparison between the proportion of male and female respondents (153) and nonrespondents (43) reveals no statistically significant difference. The two groups "prove" to be randomly drawn from a common binomial population; in essence, the respondents and nonrespondents do not differ significantly from each other with respect to sex.[1] As these two variables, position and sex, are (along with age and salary which, not being available for the nonrespondents, cannot be compared for the two groups) those most likely to affect the results, and as age is somewhat correlated with both level of position and salary, it seems highly probable that data from the nonrespondents would not substantially alter the results. It is, nonetheless, not a certainty, and the findings in this chapter are presented and should be read in that light. That is, the measures reported here might possibly be somewhat different if data were available from all 196 graduates.

Geographical Distribution

The geographical distribution of the graduates is shown in figure 3. The data substantiate the view, which is so strong as to be accepted as fact, that library school graduates tend to remain in—as they tend to be recruited from—the states or nearby regions of their schools. Location data were available for 191 graduates, of whom 26 are doctoral students and 165 are employed, 113 of them in the United States. Of these 113, only 25, or 22 percent, are located in states and the District of Columbia without sixth-year program schools; only fifteen states and the District, not having such schools, have succeeded in attracting graduates of the programs, and eleven of the fifteen states are adjacent to ones which do

[1] For the statistically minded: $X^2 = .31$. For 1 *df*, the value significant with a probability of .05 is 3.841.

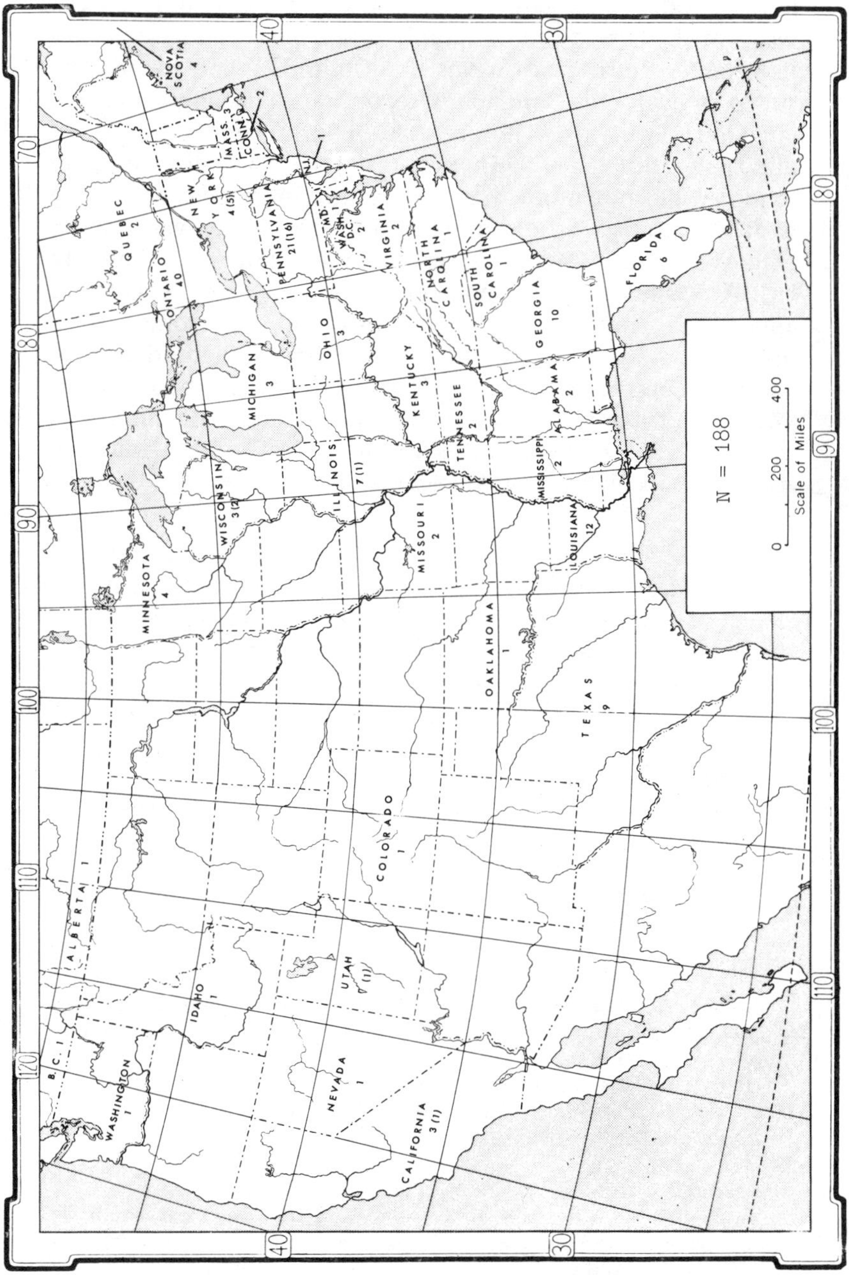

© by DENOYER-GEPPERT COMPANY, CHICAGO (Used by permission)

Fig. 3. Location of Employed Graduates

43

have schools. This can scarcely be explained simply on the basis of U.S. cultural geography, i.e., large and numerous libraries are near institutions like Columbia, and so on. The states of Colorado, Indiana, Oregon, and Washington have a large city or two, a library school, and large numbers of librarians. But they have no sixth-year specialist program schools—and not more than 1 graduate. In the entire country west of Louisiana and north of Texas there are only 8 employed sixth-year program graduates, and 3 of these are UCLA graduates. It seems probable that most larger and almost all very large libraries as well as some other institutions, such as junior college libraries, would benefit from the employment of staff members with an additional year of professional-combined-with-academic education. If this view be accepted, the establishment of a few additional sixth-year specialist program schools is indicated.

Age and Sex

The distribution of age and sex is shown in figure 4. A first point of interest is the male-female ratio of almost 1:2.5, discussed in general terms under Enrollment in chapter 3. The following comparative national data are of interest:

	Male	Female
Sixth-year graduates	29.1%	70.9%
Academic librarians*	36.4	63.5
Public librarianst	12.8	87.1
Special librarians‡	25.9	72.0
1960 census: all librarians	14.4	85.5
School librarianst	6.2	93.8
Doctoral graduates (through 1962)§	72.8	27.1

*Anita R. Schiller, *Characteristics of Professional Personnel in College and University Libraries,* Research Series no.16 (Springfield, Ill.: Illinois State Library, 1969).

†Henry T. Drennan and Richard L. Darling, *Library Manpower: Occupational Characteristics of Public and School Librarians* (Washington, D.C.: Govt. Print. Off., 1966). (Office of Education—15061)

‡*Special Libraries* 58: 251 (April 1967).

§J. Periam Danton and LeRoy C. Merritt, "Doctoral Study in Librarianship—A Supplement," *College and Research Libraries* 23: 539 - 40 (November 1962).

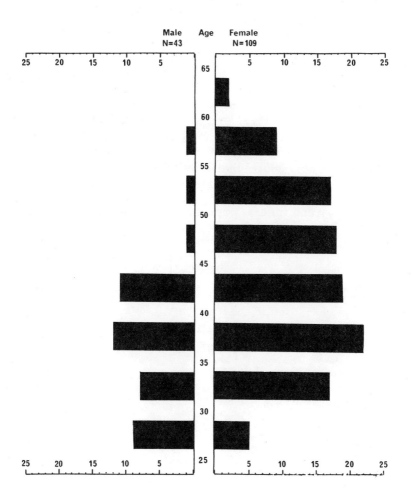

Fig. 4 Age and Sex of Graduates
N=152

It will be observed that only the academic librarians and doctoral graduates show higher ratios of men to women than do the sixth-year graduates. For the educationally most advanced group of 172 doctoral graduates (through 1962), the ratio is more than reversed: males 126, females 46, or 2.74:1.

The other principal point of interest from figure 4 is the high proportion of female graduates and the low proportion of male graduates who were over forty, forty-five, and fifty years of age. Just under 60 percent of the 109 females were over forty, 40 percent were over forty-five, and more than a quarter were over fifty. In marked contrast, fewer than one-third of the males were over forty, only 7 percent were over forty-five, and only 5 percent were over fifty. The opposite side of the coin shows that only 20 percent of the females and almost 40 percent of the males were under thirty-five.

In figures, and for easy comparison, the data are:

Age	Male	Female
Under 35	40—%	20 %
Over 40	33—	60—
Over 45	7	40+
Over 50	5	25+

Some comparative national data are as follows:

	Male		
Age	25 - 34	35 - 44	45 - 64
Sixth-year graduates	39.5%	53.4%	6.9%
Academic librarians*	28.4	32.6	35.7
Public librarians†	30.8	34.6	32.7
	Female		
Sixth-year graduates	20.1%	37.6%	42.2%
Academic librarians*	22.6	17.7	52.2
Public librarians†	12.9	21.7	56.2

*Anita R. Schiller, *Characteristics of Professional Personnel.*
†Henry T. Drennan and Richard L. Darling, *Library Manpower: Occupational Characteristics.*

All these data go a considerable distance toward substantiating the hypotheses advanced earlier, namely, that the male librarian normally from the beginning has a lifelong career in view and seeks additional education to further it and the support of his family, whereas many younger women leave the profession for marriage, and others anticipate marriage in the future; when they seek further education, therefore, they are, on the average, much older. There is also the possibility that a larger proportion of older women are using these programs as "refresher" courses, but so far as the writer is aware, there is no evidence to support a difference between the sexes in this respect.

Schools Where Sixth-Year Graduates Obtained the B.L.S./M.L.S.

All respondents reported the schools where they had obtained their B.L.S. or M.L.S. degrees, and the results are given in table 15. The main facts which the table displays are, first, that only a little over half of the accredited schools have supplied graduating students for the sixth-year programs and, second, that by and large, and in the case of some schools up to 100 percent, the graduates have done their sixth-year work at the same school where they took their first professional degree. Of these sixth-year schools which have had a substantial number of graduates, only Illinois, Louisiana, and Pittsburgh are exceptions, that is, have attracted a considerable proportion of M.L.S. graduates of other schools. Almost certainly, the prime factor of some kind of convenience has operated in both respects (see also page 52). The lesson to be drawn is that, up to the present, at least, no matter what a school does or offers, and no matter how good its program and faculty, it cannot, *generally speaking*, expect to attract to its sixth-year program a large proportion of students from other distant schools. The writer believes this to be a situation disadvantageous both to the student and to the profession since the student will be benefited, other things being more or less equal, by exposure to different faculties, ideas, and viewpoints; but rectification is not easy to suggest, or even to imagine. An increase in the size and number of a school's available fellowships plus *possibly*, but only just possibly, the building of a truly distinguished faculty of national reputation seem the only likely causes of change.

Table 15

SCHOOLS WHERE SIXTH-YEAR GRADUATES OBTAINED B.L.S./M.L.S. DEGREE
N=153

	Atlanta	Case Western	Columbia	Denver	Drexel	Emory	Florida State	Illinois	Indiana	Kentucky	Louisiana State	Mc Gill	Michigan	Minnesota	North Carolina	Peabody	Pittsburgh	Rosary	Texas	Toronto	UCLA	Washington	Western Michigan	Wisconsin	Total
Columbia			8																						
Emory						6				1						1									
Florida State[a]	1						6	1								1								2	
Illinois				2			1	5			1			1								1			
Louisiana State				1							11														
Maryland	1	1	1				1				1		1		1	3		1				1			
Minnesota				1										1	1										
Peabody																5									
Pittsburgh[a]	1			1	1								1	1		1	20						1	1	
Texas									1										3			1			
Toronto[a]												3								28					
UCLA																					3				
Western Michigan			2																						
Wisconsin		1	3								1													2	
Total	2	2	14	5	1	6	8	5	1	1	14	3	2	3	2	11	20	1	3	28	3	3	1	5	

a. Florida, Pittsburgh and Toronto, 1, 1, and 3 graduates, respectively, of unaccredited schools; Pittsburgh, 1 from Karachi; Toronto, 1 each from the University of Cape Town, Punjab University, and Aligarh University, India.

Reasons Professionally Experienced Graduates
Entered Sixth-Year Program

Well over half of the graduates who indicated their reasons for embarking upon the sixth-year program apparently felt a need for some kind of specialization in, or upgrading of, their professional equipment. The categories of table 16, which quantify the answers to the questions on this point, are clearly nondiscrete and not sharply defined in all respects. The categories of columns 5 through 8, for example, are specific kinds of the "specialization beyond the M.L.S." of column 2. Consequently, if the 122 responses under these columns are added to the 73 of column 2, it may be said that nearly half of all responses indicated entry into the program for this basic reason, however interpreted or however particularized. Two other facts are immediately apparent from the table. Nearly 30 percent of all respondents give as a reason, if not the principal reason, for further study their desire to prepare themselves for library school teaching, and 40 percent thought of the program as a possible step toward the doctorate. This is an interesting finding in view of the data shown in table 3. That is, a substantial number of those who have graduated apparently think or thought of the program as a first step toward the doctorate, even though the schools in which they have enrolled usually think of the program as a terminal one. As might be expected, a wide variety of "Other" reasons are represented by the figures in column 10 of table 16. Just over half of these responses gave a reason which might be characterized as a desire to earn more money, or to qualify for tenure or some kind of certification or status. It is not impossible that reasons of this general kind helped, more or less unconsciously, to influence some of the other graduates.

Objectives of Graduates Who Entered Sixth-Year
Program Directly

Of the 26 graduates who entered sixth-year programs directly after receiving the B.L.S./M.L.S. degree, an even larger proportion, nearly 70 percent, had as possible objective a step toward the doctorate, and an almost equally large

49

Table 16

REASONS PROFESSIONALLY EXPERIENCED GRADUATES ENTERED SIXTH-YEAR PROGRAM

N=131

Institution	Specialization Beyond M.L.S.	Update Knowledge	Upgrade Professional Skills	Special Program for Teaching Librarianship	Preparation for Administrative Work	Information and Automation Skills	Administration of Instructional Media	Step Toward Doctorate	Other	N for School
(1)	(2)	(3)	(4)	(5)	(6)	(7)	(8)	(9)	(10)	(11)
Columbia	3	6	5	5	2	3	1	3	3	8
Emory	3	5	5			2			3	7
Florida State	6	4	4	8	2	1	2	5	1	9
Illinois	6	10	10	3	2	6	1	3	5	14
Louisiana State	6	11	10	4	1	4	2	7	5	15
Maryland	3	5	3	2	2	3		4	1	5
Minnesota	1	1	1	1						1
Peabody	3	4	4	5				1		4
Pittsburgh	13	12	10	5	9	14	4	21	3	24
Texas	2	3	1	2			2			3
Toronto	23	20	24	3	13	5		7	7	33
UCLA										
Western Michigan		2	2	2		2		2		2
Wisconsin	4	3	3	2		1	1	2	1	6
Total	73	86	82	37	31	41	13	53	29	131

Note: More than one category checked by some respondents.

number viewed the sixth-year program as an avenue for securing specialization they did not receive in their M.L.S. programs. The data here, shown in table 17, fortify those of table 16 by suggesting both the validity of the whole specialization concept and the thought that at least some of the schools should probably pay more attention than they have to possible or potential interest in the doctorate.

Table 17
OBJECTIVE OF GRADUATES WHO ENTERED SIXTH-YEAR PROGRAM
DIRECTLY AFTER B.L.S./M.L.S. DEGREE
N=26

Institution (1)	Change in Career Interest (2)	Secure Specialization Not Received With M.L.S. (3)	Possible Step Toward Doctorate (4)	Other (5)	N = for School (6)
Columbia		1	1	1	1
Emory					
Florida State					
Illinois					
Louisiana State		2	2		3
Maryland					
Minnesota					
Peabody		1			1
Pittsburgh	3	3	10	4	11
Texas		3	2	1	3
Toronto	1	2	3	1	4
UCLA		3			3
Western Michigan					
Wisconsin					
Total	4	15	18	7	26

Note: More than one category checked by some respondents.

"Other":
Columbia: "To be better prepared to teach ... enrichment of background."
Pittsburgh: "To take advantage of tuition reduction." "Wanted to try teaching." "To qualify for promotion to higher faculty rank and salary," etc.
Texas: "I wanted to try teaching in this program to see how I liked it and whether I would ... need a Ph.D. ..."
Toronto: "Because of my feelings that this was simply part of an academic (professional) education."

Reasons Graduates Chose Sixth-Year Program School

The particular reason(s) graduates chose the sixth-year program school they did are displayed in table 18. A total of 389 "reason-responses" were given, or an average of a little more than two and a half responses per graduate. It will not surprise anyone familiar with patterns of library school recruitment to learn that the response most frequently cited—60 percent of the total—was that of "convenience," that is, proximity to home, position, and the like. Much of this factor of "convenience" is no doubt correlated with the

Table 18
REASONS GRADUATES CHOSE PARTICULAR SIXTH-YEAR
SPECIALIST PROGRAM SCHOOL
N=152

Institution	Same School Received M.L.S.	Different School from M.L.S.	Convenience Near Home, Job, etc.	Curriculum Offered	Reputation of the Faculty	Reputation of the School	Reputation of the University	Offered Fellowship	Other	N for School
(1)	(2)	(3)	(4)	(5)	(6)	(7)	(8)	(9)	(10)	(11)
Columbia	3		5	2	6	7	2	1	1	8
Emory	3		7	1	2	3	4			7
Florida State	1	3	5	5	4	5	2	2		9
Illinois		4	5	5	4	8	8		6	14
Louisiana State	3	1	13	2	3	4	5	5	1	18
Maryland		1	2		1	1		3		5
Minnesota		1	1					1		1
Peabody	5		2	3	1	2				5
Pittsburgh	8	2	23	9	9	6	5	1	5	32
Texas	1		5	1	3	2	2	1		5
Toronto	4	3	27	11	9	20	21	1	3	36
UCLA	2		1	3	1	2	1			3
Western Michigan				2	2	2			1	2
Wisconsin	2	1	3	2	1	1	4	1		7
Total	32	16	99	46	46	63	54	16	17	152

Note: More than one category checked by some respondents.
"Other":
Columbia: "I like New York City."
Illinois: "In state--helpful for tuition--some courses offered in extension."
"Because I was aware of its sixth-year program."
"Illinois was one of few schools to give certificate in 1964-65."
"First school known to me that offered sixth-year," etc.
Louisiana State: "They asked me to apply."
Pittsburgh: "Company was willing to pay full costs."
"School also offers Ph.D."
"I am in the Ph.D. program at Pitt. and was eligible for the Adv. Cert. after completing 24 semester hours credit."
Toronto: "Summer sessions. Univ. of Toronto only school giving sixth-year masters in 1964." "Part-time program."
Western Michigan: "Because degree instead of certificate is offered."

responses under column 2, since we know that most M.L.S.-degree students come from the state in which the school is located. The 16 graduates who gave the receipt of a fellowship as their reason for choice of school also made their choice on a personal rather than on a school-related basis.

Only 12 percent of the responses named "reputation of the faculty" and only 16 percent "reputation of the school" as a reason for going to the particular institution they did. These figures may not be surprising, but they are smaller than the percentage resulting from the great drawing power of a distinguished faculty/department of history, anthropology, or education at the postmaster's level. The figures may be viewed as somewhat discouraging, therefore, from the point of view that, as of the present, no matter how able and distinguished a library school and its faculty may be, it is likely to draw only a small proportion of its students from afar, and its reputation does not to a great extent outweigh the factor of convenience in the prospective student's choice of his school. This finding is very closely related to and supports that of table 15.

Graduates' Long-Range Career Plans

The long-range career plans of the graduates, shown in table 19, are instructive in the light of the findings of table 17 and table 20, discussed below. The plans, as the graduates now view them, should also be of considerable interest to present and prospective sixth-year program schools. The 149 respondents in table 19 checked a total of 214 possible career objectives, or a little fewer than 1.5 responses per graduate. Library school teaching, mentioned 81 times, or nearly 40 percent of all responses, is far and away in first place. Various levels of professional activity (columns 4 through 8) in all kinds of libraries except those of schools and junior colleges, taken together, yield only 97 responses.

The responses under "other" (column 10) are almost as varied as their number and represent such comments as "I would consider any of the above checked categories and have not definitely chosen my ultimate goal"; "work with A.I.D. or other agencies in Latin American libraries"; "consultant or in-service training officer, probably for a state agency"; "I

Table 19
GRADUATES' LONG-RANGE CAREER PLANS
N=149

Institution	School Librarianship*	Junior College Librarian	Chief or Assistant Librarian, "Medium-Level" Library	"Middle-Level" Administration, Major Library	Chief or Assistant Librarian, Major Library	Subject Specialist, Major Library	Special Collections Librarian	Special Library School Teaching	Other	N for School
(1)	(2)	(3)	(4)	(5)	(6)	(7)	(8)	(9)	(10)	(11)
Columbia	3			1				7	2	8
Emory	5		2	1						7
Florida State	3			1				6	1	9
Illinois	1	1	4	2	2			6	3	14
Louisiana State	1	2	1	4	2	4	1	11		18
Maryland				1		2	2	4		5
Minnesota								1		1
Peabody	1				1			2		4
Pittsburgh	1		1	5	6	8	4	21	4	31
Texas				2	1	1	1	4	1	5
Toronto	1		3	9	9	5	4	12	3	35
UCLA	1			1		1	2	1		3
Western Michigan								2		2
Wisconsin	1			1	1			4	1	7
Total	18	3	12	28	22	21	14	81	15	149

Note: More than one category checked by some respondents.

* Includes: School library administration and supervision of instructional media centers.

have no long-range career plans"; and "I serve only as a consultant in the library field now." The small amount of interest in any aspect of school librarianship seems a little surprising and somewhat discouraging—surprising in view of the number of specializations and courses which have been developed for this field.

At least one other finding of table 19 is of interest, namely, that less than 30 percent of all the respondents evidenced interest in upper-level administrative responsibility in larger libraries of any kind (columns 4 through 6). Possible causes of this finding escape the writer, but its principal implications appear to be, first, that the graduates really did enter the sixth-year program to secure some kind of specialization, rather than with the aim of achieving higher level administrative posts, and, second, that such posts may not be so attractive to graduates as has sometimes been anticipated.

Employment

Table 20, which shows type of employment of the graduates in spring 1969 as reported by the schools, reveals little of surprise. More than 45 percent of all graduates are in college and university libraries. In second place, with 22.5 percent, is library school teaching, and there is a three-way tie between employment in public libraries, school libraries, and special libraries. In view of the great shortages in the field, the gratifying figure is undoubtedly the 36 individuals who are library school teachers; they represent a far higher proportion than is the case for M.L.S. graduates.[2] However, the figure is not entirely surprising in light of the fact (table 2) that at least eight of the twenty schools have or had "programs for teaching librarianship" as a specific specialization, for which, it may be noted, HEW fellowships are particularly intended.

If table 20 is in any way surprising, it is so in the large number of graduates, almost 44 percent, who have remained

[2] Only 27, or less than 1 percent, of the 3,571 library school graduates of 1968 were employed as library school teachers. College and university libraries employed 1,254, or 35 percent. See Carlyle J. Frarey and Richard S. Rosenstein, "Placement and Salary Picture in 1968 . . .," *Library Journal* 94: 2427 - 28 (15 June 1969).

Table 20
EMPLOYMENT OF GRADUATES*
N=161

Institution (1)	Public Libraries (2)	School Libraries (3)	Coll. and Univ. Libraries (4)	Special Libraries (5)	Lib. School Teaching (6)	Total (7)	Position in Same Library** (8)
Columbia							
Emory	2	5				7	7
Florida State	1		3		4	8	4
Illinois		1	13		1	15	12
Louisiana State	3	3	7		6	19	6
Maryland			3	1	1	5	3
Minnesota					1	1	
Peabody	1	4	1		3	9	5
Pittsburgh	1	2	18	5	5	31	12
Texas			3	1	1	5	
Toronto	7	1	23	9	10	50	17
UCLA	2		1			3	
Western Michigan		1			2	3	1
Wisconsin		1	1	1	2	5	2
Total	17	18	73	17	36	161	69

 * Based upon returns from the schools; excludes doctoral students.
** Of the graduates who previously held library positions, number who have
   remained in or returned to a position in the same library.

in the same institution—though not, of course, necessarily in the same position—they were in when they embarked upon sixth-year study. The implications of this fact are neither quantifiable nor wholly clear. In some cases, obviously, need or desire for state certification or credential in the library of employment prior to the sixth-year program has been a factor. The desire to advance within the system is almost certainly the explanation for some. Probably the fact that a library has itself embarked upon a new program—as, for example, automated records—has caused some of its employees to be induced to prepare themselves for the new procedure. In any case, it is clear that for 69 librarians, at least, the potential attraction of greener pastures in another institution was not their reason for embarking upon the sixth-year specialist program.

Table 21 describes the employment of graduates in another way by showing their movement from one kind of library to another. (As the data in this table are based upon responses from the graduates, the figures are different from those of table 20, which is based upon data supplied by the schools, but the percentages of the two tables are very similar.) Table 21 is to be read as follows: of 18 graduates who were employed in public libraries, 6 remained in that field, 1 went to a school library, 5 to college or university libraries, 2 to special libraries, and 4 to library school teaching. It will be seen that the types of employment which lost the most graduates, proportionately, were the public and the school

Table 21
NUMBER OF GRADUATES WHO WENT FROM ONE TYPE OF LIBRARY TO
ANOTHER AFTER SIXTH-YEAR PROGRAM*
N=135
PRESENT POSITION

Previous Position (1)	Public Library (2)	School Library (3)	College or University Library (4)	Special Library (5)	State Library (6)	Library School Teaching (7)	Other-- in Field of Librarianship (8)	Non-Library Work (9)	Total (10)
Public Library	6	1	5	2		4			18
School Library	1	18	1		2	8	1		31
University or College Library	2		38	2		7		2	51
Special Library				3					3
State Library			1		1	2			4
Library School Teaching					1	6			7
Other-- in Field of Librarianship		1	1				1		3
No Previous Employment in Library Reported	3	3	8	1		2		1	18
Total	12	23	54	8	4	29	2	3	135

* Based upon returns from graduates. Of 153 respondents, fifteen were currently doctoral students and three not employed.

library; library school teaching and the academic and special library gained. Generally speaking, however, there was considerable fidelity to previous type of employment. This suggests a certain amount of inherent resistance to, or difficulty in, mobility of the kind under discussion. Whether this is advantageous or not is probably arguable, but the apparent fact is one which both schools and students might do well to bear in mind in shaping their plans.

Information was also secured from the graduates who had been previously employed concerning change, if any, in *type* of position. However, after the responses had been examined and analyzed, it was determined that the changes recorded could not be synthesized or generalized upon in any meaningful way. The validity of this statement can perhaps best be made clear by citing a number of the actual changes: Department Head to Consultant to the Director; Assistant Book Order Librarian to Head of the Reference Department, Undergraduate Library; Campus School Librarian to Assistant Professor, Library School; Supervisor, Instructional Materials, to Director, Educational Media; Head, Reference Department, to Book Selection Coordinator; Assistant Librarian to Assistant Professor, Library School; Assistant Reference Librarian to General Science Librarian; Reference Librarian to Curriculum Librarian; Head, Public Services, to Head, Social Sciences; Cataloger to Head, East Asia Section. These changes, representative of all, form no pattern.

Previous and Present Salaries of Graduates with Experience

The data in table 22 derived from a question which asked graduates who had had professional experience before entering the sixth-year program to indicate whether their present salaries were higher, about the same as, or lower than their previous ones. The "same" was defined as a difference of not more than $300. For the results to be really discriminating, the figure should probably have been set considerably higher, since almost any librarian performing satisfactorily may expect an increment of at least this size every year or two even without a change of position or further study. All that table 22 tells us for certain, therefore, is that 97, or

58

Table 22
SALARY OF PRESENT POSITION COMPARED WITH THAT OF
PREVIOUS POSITION
N=119

Institution (1)	Higher (2)	Same (3)	Lower (4)	N for School (5)
Columbia	4	2		6
Emory	7			7
Florida State	7	1		8
Illinois	12	2		14
Louisiana State	10	3	1	14
Maryland	1	4		5
Minnesota	1			1
Peabody	4			4
Pittsburgh	17	3		20
Texas	1			1
Toronto	28	5		33
UCLA				
Western Michigan	1	1		2
Wisconsin	4			4
Total	97	21	1	119
Percentage	81.5	17.6	.8	99.9

about 81 percent, of the 119 reporting graduates previously and currently employed are now receiving salaries more than $300 higher than those they had. It would probably be cause for wonderment and concern if this were not the case.

Of 116 U.S. respondents, 14 are doctoral students, 28 either were not employed before the sixth-year program or reported only one salary, and 1 is employed abroad. The remaining 73 gave information on their "before" and "after" salaries. The data are shown in figure 5. The "before" and "after" means and medians for the men and women are as follows:

	Men		Women	
	Before	After	Before	After
Mean	7,556	11,277	8,346	10,636
Median	7,759	11,045	8,433	10,340

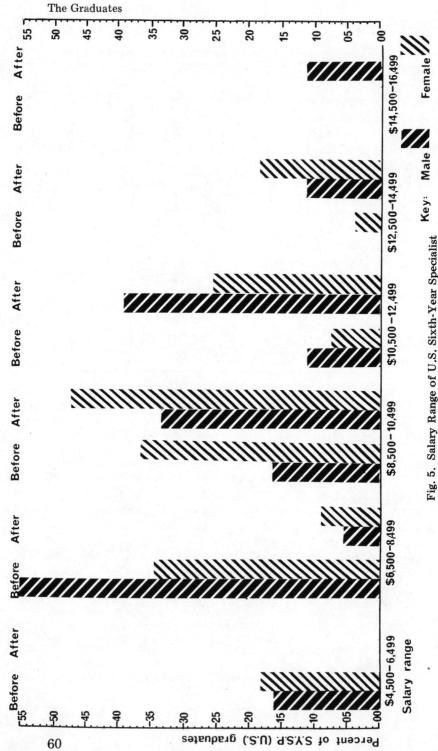

Fig. 5. Salary Range of U.S. Sixth-Year Specialist
Program Graduates before and after Sixth Year

N=73

Key:　Male　Female

Percent of S.Y.S.P. (U.S.) graduates

Salary range

60

There is no point here in determining whether the differences between the means are statistically significant, since some of the differences are unquestionably due to normal merit increases, promotions, and changes in responsibility and position. Further, it would be impossible to select a provably similar control group, determine what its salary increase over the same number of years had been, and then examine the salary differences between this group and the graduates. All one can say is that it is extremely unlikely that, *on average*, librarians would, within one to three years, have received salaries higher by $2,000 to $3,700. Some of this increase is, therefore, almost certainly the result of graduation from the sixth-year programs.

Figure 5 reveals, among other things, that no men or women were in the lowest salary range after graduation, and that only 6 percent of the men and 11 percent of the women were in the second-lowest, whereas before the sixth-year program the percentages were 54 and 29, respectively. At the other end of the scale, no men and only 3 percent of the women had received salaries at or above $12,500 before taking the advanced program; after graduation, 26 percent of the men and 23 percent of the women were at this level.

It is instructive to compare the data of table 22 with those of table 23, which show that only 63, or 53 percent, of 118 reporting graduates consider the level of professional responsibility of their present position higher than that of their previous one. A higher level would, in most instances, mean "significantly" higher salary, and the data in table 23 are, therefore, more meaningful than those in table 22. It should be noted that a number of the 51 respondents of table 23 who report their level of responsibility as being the "same" are teachers who, though they may have higher rank and salary than they had, have no greater responsibility, and the same observation is probably true for some other kinds of position, e.g., subject specialists, which, though "better" and better-paid, do not entail increased responsibility. Although it is obviously not possible to say that all those who are now in positions of higher responsibility hold their present posts as a result of having attended sixth-year programs, it is certain from the accompanying internal evidence of question-

Table 23
LEVEL OF PROFESSIONAL RESPONSIBILITY OF PRESENT POSITION
COMPARED WITH THAT OF PREVIOUS POSITION
N=118

Institution (1)	Higher (2)	Same (3)	Lower (4)	N for School (5)
Columbia	4	1	1	6
Emory	2	4	1	7
Florida State	5	3		8
Illinois	4	10		14
Louisiana State	7	6	1	14
Maryland	1	4		5
Minnesota	1			1
Peabody	2	1	1	4
Pittsburgh	8	12		20
Texas	1			1
Toronto	23	9		32
UCLA				
Western Michigan	2			2
Wisconsin	3	1		4
Total	63	51	4	118
Percentage	53.3	43.2	3.3	99.8

naire responses that many do so and that, in fact, many attended the sixth-year programs with an eye toward securing a higher position.

Chapter 5 | Evaluation

The investigator of a program such as the present one knows that the most important, and by far the most difficult, question he must try to answer is, in four short words, "How good is it?" It does not seem to the writer enough to say, simply, that the faculties, book collections, facilities, and curricula of all the sixth-year specialist program schools have been studied, that they have all been accredited, and that what they do must, therefore, be at least satisfactory. The facts are, of course, that the sixth-year programs are everywhere a relatively new and experimental development and that these programs have not hitherto been examined, much less accredited. Properly to evaluate the sixth-year programs would require the same kind and degree of study and visitation that the ad hoc committees of the Committee on Accreditation devote to schools under consideration. Scrutiny of this kind was not possible for the present study. Nonetheless, an attempt is made here to provide a kind of overall estimate and evaluation which may be of benefit to the general reader as well as to the schools, prospective students, and the C.O.A.

The first basis for evaluation are the questions addressed to the graduates (Appendix C, questions 14 through 17). The second basis are the answers to a free-response question addressed to employers (Appendix D). The third is the educational attainment of the instructional staffs. These three sorts of evidence are discussed below.

Critiques from the Graduates

Of the 153 usable questionnaires from graduates, all but 3 indicated the degree of satisfaction the respondents felt with their sixth-year programs. The responses are summarized in table 24. If the sums of columns 2 and 3 are added, it is seen that 76, or half of the group, felt "Extremely Satisfied" or "Well Satisfied." Similarly, if the sums of columns 5 and 6 are added, 35, or nearly one-quarter of the respondents, were "Dissatisfied" or "Extremely Dissatisfied." These statistics seem something less than gratifying. To be sure, the entries for each school are almost all small, and firm conclusions can

Table 24
DEGREE OF SATISFACTION WITH SIXTH-YEAR PROGRAMS
N=150

Institution (1)	Extremely Satisfied (2)	Well Satisfied (3)	Content (4)	Dissatisfied (5)	Extremely Dissatisfied (6)	(2)+(3) as % of (9) (7)	(5)+(6) as % of (9) (8)	N = for School (9)
Columbia		4	3	1		50.0	12.5	8
Emory	2	2	2	1		57.1	14.2	7
Florida State	2	5	1	1		77.7	11.1	9
Illinois	1	7	2	4		57.1	28.5	14
Louisiana State	4	2	5	4	2	35.2	35.2	17
Maryland		1	1	3		20.0	60.0	5
Minnesota		1				100.0	0.0	1
Peabody	1	2	2			60.0	0.0	5
Pittsburgh	4	12	7	8	1	50.0	28.1	32
Texas		2	1	2		40.0	40.0	5
Toronto	3	13	12	6	1	45.7	20.0	35
UCLA	3					100.0	0.0	3
Western Michigan	1	1				100.0	0.0	2
Wisconsin		3	3		1	42.8	14.3	7
Total	21	55	39	30	5	50.6	23.3	150

hardly be drawn from them. The fact that 3 graduates of a total graduating group of 5, say, expressed themselves as "Satisfied" is not necessarily a cause for jubilation on the part of the school, any more than it should be *necessarily* distressed if 3 of the 5 expressed themselves as being "Dissatisfied." The next 5 graduates might well express opposite views. All kinds of personal considerations, having nothing to do with the quality of the programs or the faculty, may contribute to dissatisfaction. Further, if the "Content" group of table 24 is added to the "Extremely Satisfied" and "Well Satisfied" groups, it is seen that 115, or nearly 77 percent, of the graduates have at least somewhat favorable views of their programs. It must be remembered, again, that the programs are mostly of recent origin and that they are still to a considerable extent experimental.

Nonetheless, we have here the estimates of nearly 80 percent of all graduates, and viewed from that fact the findings are somewhat disturbing. Some of the causes, at least, have just been implied. Further, some students did not really know what they were getting into. Many who expected or hoped for highly practical instruction found themselves involved in large amounts of independent study. More frequently, exactly the opposite situation obtained. Some felt that the content or extent of the program was overstated or overimplied. More specific criticisms are discussed below. What chiefly emerges from all this is the recommendation that the schools state, and publicize widely, precisely what it is they are offering, what the student may expect, and what will be expected of him. At the least, if may be suggested that those schools, the programs of which rated a low proportion of satisfaction or a high proportion of dissatisfaction, review their procedures, including student counseling and the nature of the information they disseminate.

The graduates were also provided with an opportunity to indicate the extent to which they felt the sixth-year programs prepared them for their present positions. Their responses are summarized in table 25. As one would expect, there is a high degree of consistency between the data of this table and those of table 24. Addition of the sums of columns 2 and 3 in table 25 yields a figure of 79, or about 59 percent of the respondents (column 10 − column 7 = 134), who expressed

Table 25
EXTENT TO WHICH SIXTH-YEAR PROGRAMS PREPARED GRADUATES FOR PRESENT POSITIONS
N=139

Institution (1)	Extreme- ly Well (2)	Fairly Well (3)	Ade- quate- ly (4)	Not Very Well[a] (5)	Very Poor- ly (6)	Other[b] (7)	(2)+(3) as % of (10)-(7) (8)	(5)+(6) as % of (10)-(7) (9)	N for School (10)
Columbia	1	4	2				71.4	0.0	7
Emory	3	1	1	1		1	66.6	16.6	7
Florida State	3	4	1				87.5	0.0	8
Illinois	1	7	2	2	2		57.1	28.5	14
Louisiana State	5	4	5	2	1		52.9	17.6	17
Maryland			4			1	0.0	0.0	5
Minnesota		1					100.0	0.0	1
Peabody	2	1	1	1			60.0	20.0	5
Pittsburgh	6	11	5	5	1	1	60.7	21.4	29
Texas		1		1		1	50.0	50.0	3
Toronto	3	15	7	5	3		54.5	24.2	33
UCLA	2					1	100.0	0.0	3
Western Michigan	2						100.0	0.0	2
Wisconsin	1	1	2				40.0	20.0	5
Total	29	50	30	18	7	5	59.0	18.6	139

a One respondent who checked the "Not Very Well" category noted, "It was not intended to do any-thing beyond addition of 24 graduate credits."

b Listed on page 67 of text.

themselves as having had programs which prepared them "Extremely Well" or "Fairly Well" for their present positions. If the "Adequately" group of column 4 is added, a total of 109, or 81 percent, felt themselves to be adequately or better than adequately prepared. The sum of columns 5 and 6 yields a figure of 25, or about 19 percent, who felt themselves "Not Very Well" or "Very Poorly" prepared. The difference between the proportion (18.6 percent) of this last group and the corresponding one (23.3 percent "Dissatified" or "Extremely Dissatisfied") of table 24 is to a considerable extent explained by the fact that, for one reason or another, some of the graduates accepted positions having nothing to do with the specialization programs they took, that is, positions for which the programs were not designed to prepare them. "Other" answers in table 25 included:

> The program was not even relevant. My present position uses only a fraction of my library skills.

> I still cannot find a job to practice what I learned about library automation.

> Present job based on convenience to husband's job and bears little relationship to content of advanced course . . . so answer is not a fair evaluation of program.

> Actually, I am overprepared for my present position— or perhaps I should say that my present position requires no training beyond the M.L.S. degree!

> I accepted a position . . . totally unrelated to my 6th-year program.

Nonetheless, the findings of table 25 are about as disturbing as those of table 24, and the comment and suggestions offered on the latter apply also to the former.

Questions 14 through 17 of the questionnaire to graduates (Appendix C) evoked a very large number of free responses, all of them exceedingly frank and some quite bitter. The graduates' comment on all four questions is here summarized.

The most frequently cited suggestions and adverse criticisms, in order of frequency, were the need for: (1) (more) courses, beyond the M.L.S. level, specifically for sixth-year program students; (2) improvement of the faculty, either in educational attainment or in teaching quality; (3) updating, or making more relevant, parts of the curriculum; (4) more independent or research-oriented study; (5) more specialized courses; (6) more course work in information science; (7) specific recognition of and reward for the sixth-year programs by libraries; and (8) a degree or diploma as award for satisfactory completion of the program.

Several points should be made concerning these comments: (1) none of the criticisms is voiced by as many as a fifth of the responding graduates; (2) when spread, as they are, among the schools, the absolute numbers of specific criticisms for a particular school are small; (3) some of the criticisms, coming from graduates of earlier years, are no longer valid; most programs a few years old have been improved since their establishment; (4) certain of the criticisms (see, for example, page 67) clearly apply, not to the schools and library education, but rather to libraries and the employment situation. Nonetheless, the criticisms, amounting in total to nearly a hundred, constitute a fairly considerable dissatisfaction with and indictment of at least some aspects of some programs. This is unquestionably the impression gained by anyone reading through the detailed, circumstantial, and often lengthy critiques written by the graduates; many are concerned, unhappy—and desirous of seeing, and contributing to, improvement. No school totally escaped negative criticism. It is suggested, therefore, again, that the schools review their programs in the light of such of the school-directed criticisms as are, or may possibly be, applicable to them.

Not all criticism was negative. Twenty-nine graduates offered favorable comment, but it seems significant that 9, or almost a third of these, dealt only with the respondents' gratification at having been able to take courses outside the library school, and 4 others with freedom of course choice. Three praised the quality of teaching, and 2 others an individual faculty member. Other favorable comments, none mentioned more than once, had to do with guest lecturers, imaginative curriculum, the general idea of the sixth-year program, concern with the individual student, and the gaining of "new insights."

The Employers

The institutional employers of the graduates were analyzed and discussed in the preceding chapter. It was the belief of the writer that one basis for evaluation of the contribution which the sixth-year specialist programs were making might be assessments from the graduates' personal employers, that is, their superior officers. Consequently, a letter (Appendix D) was sent to 70 identifiable individuals in the United States representing a total of 83 graduates. The occupational status of these 70, and the extent to which they responded to the letter, are shown in table 26.

Table 26
DISTRIBUTION OF EMPLOYERS

Employers (1)	Number of Letters Sent (2)	Number of Replies Received (3)	Percentage of Replies Received (3) ÷ (2) (4)
Public and County Librarians	2	2	100.0
Academic Librarians	32	20	62.5
Library School Deans	15	11	73.3
College Presidents	9	3	33.3
Special Librarians	4	2	50.0
State Librarians	4	3	75.0
Other	4	4	100.0
Total	70	45	64.3

The percentage of responses (64.3) is good enough. There is no reason to believe that the nonrespondents differ in any significant respect from those who responded. However, there are several considerations which militated against the ability of respondents to reply meaningfully and, hence, against the usefulness of the replies. For one thing, it is seldom, if ever, possible for the superior officer completely to isolate from other factors, such as personal qualifications and basic library education, the contribution which the sixth-year program itself has made to the employee's competence and performance. A number of respondents mentioned this point. In the second place, as shown in the previous chapter, some graduates either were employed for the first time after their advanced study, or were employed in institutions different from those which had previously employed them. Consequently, the employer had no yardstick against which to measure the contribution of the sixth-year program.

Finally, the nature of employment was, in some cases, such that the potential benefit of the program was not directly relevant. (A most disheartening reply in this connection came from a state college librarian who wrote: "I . . . feel that most of the work [being done by the sixth-year graduate] is clerical in nature and could be done by a clerk or library assistant." It is no wonder that the profession has recruiting problems.) These several considerations were, of course, all recognized in advance, but it was nonetheless thought worthwhile to attempt to secure such opinions and judgments as might be obtained. The results of this effort are worthy of reporting; they are summarized below.

For one or another of the reasons noted at the beginning of this section, 8 of the 45 responding employers were unable to provide any evaluation of their sixth-year graduates. The responses of the remaining 37 may be broadly summarized as follows, with more than half of the respondents supplying opinion in more than one of the categories; the indicated number of graduates is also, therefore, not discrete: (1) 16 employers, employing 18 graduates, wrote in strong, affirmative terms of the general value of sixth-year programs and endorsed the concept; (2) 19 employers (24 graduates) believed that the *individuals* involved had been somewhat to very greatly benefited by the programs; (3) 26 employers (28 graduates) believed that the programs had been of some to "immeasurable" benefit to the *positions* the graduates held; (4) 5 employers (5 graduates) raised some question as to either the general or the specific value of the programs, and 2 of these believed them to be of little value; and (5) 2 respondents specifically suggested that either experience or personal qualifications was more valuable. While these figures are not large, they do display a highly favorable employer reaction involving 52 graduates, or almost 47 percent of all U.S. employed graduates.

Educational Attainment of the Instructional Staffs

Presumably it need not be argued here that a major element, if not *the* major element, in the quality of any educational program is the excellence of the teaching corps. This excellence is, of course, made up of many factors: personality; knowledge of the subject; ability to present it logically and clearly; ability to gain rapport with students; teaching method; and, closely related to knowledge of the subject, educational attainment, among others. All but the last of these are exceedingly difficult to measure and, some would say, almost impossible to assess in objective and meaningful terms. Educational attainment can, however, be determined, and some attention is paid to this point here.

According to the latest announcements and other information from the twenty schools, their instructional staffs total(ed) approximately 161 full-time and 48 part-time holders of the B.L.S./M.L.S. degree; 17 full-time and 1 part-time holders of a sixth-year degree or certificate; 4 full-time and 9 part-time holders of a subject master's degree; and 87 full-time and 12 part-time holders of an earned doctorate. Several aspects of these findings are of interest.

In the first place, there is the astonishingly large number (161) of library school instructors who hold no degree higher than the B.L.S./M.L.S. Of full-time faculty, almost 60 percent are in this group. While it cannot always be determined who teaches what, it is absolutely certain that many of these instructors are teaching sixth-year students—and a few of them, at least, are teaching at the doctoral level. It is the view of the writer—and of a considerable number of sixth-year program graduates—that this practice is *in general* a mistake. It is commonly accepted in American education that the instructor should, by and large, have achieved a higher level of educational attainment than those whom he instructs: the high school teacher should have at least a college education, the college instructor should normally have at least a master's degree, and those who teach at the master's or doctoral level should themselves have the doctorate. The sixth-year schools appear not to have held very closely to this tenet. In view of the fact that all but three or four of the accredited schools generally considered strongest are in the sixth-year program group, and the further fact that a number of the schools that would generally be held to be weakest are not, it seems reasonable to suggest that the situation in the accredited schools as a group is probably as bad as and may be worse than that in the sixth-year schools just described.

A second point of interest is the relatively small number (17) of sixth-year graduates employed full-time as instructors in the sixth-year program schools. Only half of the twenty schools employ(ed) these graduates, and just over half of the 17 graduates are employed in two schools, Pittsburgh and Toronto. Only one other school, apparently, employs or employed more than 1. At least four of the schools which employ no sixth-year graduates also have on their staffs 2 or fewer holders of the doctorate. These several findings seem to suggest, first, that schools with sixth-year programs should give thought to the employment of more graduates of these programs and, second, that most of the schools should give serious consideration to the upgrading of the educational attainment of their instructional staffs, most especially, of those members who teach at and beyond the M.L.S. level.

Many of the schools, and not only those with doctoral programs, indicate that they need to find people with the doctorate in making new faculty appointments—a viewpoint which the writer applauds. The fact is, however, that most of the schools are appointing and/or retaining on their faculties large numbers of full-time instructors who have only the B.L.S./M.L.S. degree. Other things being equal, it would clearly be better for the schools to appoint sixth-year program graduates instead.

On the favorable side is the substantial number of instructors with the doctorate—87, or nearly one-third, of the full-time faculty. Only one school has none, four have 2, and the mean is a very respectable 4.4. This is a great improvement over the situation which existed a generation ago. At that time, only 27, or a little over 18 percent, of 148 full-time faculty in *all* the thirty-two schools then accredited held the doctor's degree; but, on the other hand, only one school then offered a program for the degree.[1]

[1] J. Periam Danton, *Education for Librarianship: Criticisms, Dilemmas, and Proposals* (New York: Columbia Univ. School of Library Service, 1946), p.10.

The writer has played devil's advocate in reporting, as fully as the facts warranted, negative (as well, of course, as positive) critiques of the sixth-year specialist programs. In brief summary of this chapter, as well as of some material presented earlier, it is his conviction that:

1. The basic concept of the sixth-year program is sound, and the idea should be supported and encouraged.

2. A large majority of the present programs are viable, will continue, and will probably improve qualitatively and expand quantitatively. (This conclusion is based upon general enrollment and graduation trends, and information supplied by, and discussions held with, the deans/directors and some faculty members of the schools.)

3. A majority, probably a strong majority, of the programs are functioning reasonably well to excellently.

4. Most programs can be, and a few need to be, improved in one or more respects. (See Recommendations in the following chapter.)

Chapter 6	# Summary and Recommendations

The present study was commissioned September 1968; preliminary work was begun December 1968; the study was completed and report submitted September 1969.

Summary

Chapter 1. Background of the Sixth-Year Specialist Program

A brief historical overview was given of formal library education, with special reference to accreditation and to the two-year master's degree programs which existed from 1927 to 1960. The relationship was shown of these programs to the so-called sixth-year specialist programs, which more or less formally began in 1961. The two appear to differ most significantly in that the old two-year master's programs were a general, across-the-board, advanced curriculum, whereas the sixth-year specialist programs are intended to provide preparation for a particular (specialized) kind of professional activity.

Chapter 2. Scope and Method of the Study

A sixth-year specialist program was deemed to be in effect if a school had somewhat formally established a plan and program, given it a label, stated a purpose or purposes, and set up requirements for admission to and completion of the work.

Data were secured through questionnaires sent to all the accredited library schools and through visits to most of those having sixth-year specialist programs; through questionnaires sent to all the 196 graduates of such programs; through discussions with deans, faculty members, students, and graduates of the schools; and from letters from employers of graduates.

Chapter 3. The Schools

Twenty schools have or have had sixth-year specialist programs, three programs being inoperative as of 1968 - 69. All but two schools, Texas and UCLA, lie east of the Mississippi. Three-quarters of the schools began their programs after 1965; only three began before 1963. All the schools conceive of their programs as ones that would provide for at least some kind of *specialization* beyond the M.L.S. degree, with more than a third of the schools still operating programs having teaching of librarianship as a specific specialization.

Of the thirteen schools which, as of June 1969, had doctoral programs, nine had sixth-year specialist programs. Four of these nine consider the sixth-year program "terminal," or an alternative to the doctorate; two consider it terminal or a first step toward the doctorate; one considers it an alternative or a first step; one considers it a first step; and the view of the ninth suggests that the program is considered about the same as a terminal activity. Ten additional library schools are in various stages of discussion or planning leading to the possible establishment of sixth-year programs.

With only one exception, the schools require the M.L.S. degree or its equivalent for admission to the programs; three-quarters of the schools require professional experience; four-fifths set no age limit; a third set no grade point average requirement; and about half have a Graduate Record Examination requirement.

The schools have set up curricula which are highly flexible and in very large part individually tailored to the needs of the student and the particular specialization upon which he has entered. Half of the schools have developed new courses for their programs, and at least half a dozen other schools are planning such courses. Course work in other disciplines is universally encouraged.

There has been an almost steady and overall substantial enrollment increase from 1960 - 61 (9 students) to 1968 - 69 (216 students), with a high figure of 265 enrollees in 1967 - 68. Total enrollment through 1967 - 68 is composed of 223 males and 442 females, a ratio of almost 1:2 and a substantially higher proportion of males than that which obtains in the profession at large on the North American continent.

Increases in the number of graduates are also steady and substantial, from 2 in 1961 to 77 in 1968. However, two schools, Toronto with 52 and Pittsburgh with 44, account for almost 50 percent of the 196 graduates; nine schools have graduated 10 or fewer; seven schools have graduated 7 or fewer. The student attrition rate—665 total enrollees with only 196 total graduates—is deemed to be disturbingly high.

For graduation the schools require a full year of study and, in general, attainment of a B average. Fewer than half the schools require a thesis or a research project, an omission which, in view of the fact that 40 percent of all graduates consider the sixth-year program a possible first step toward the doctorate, and a considerable number of graduates do immediately or later enter upon doctoral study, may be a curricular and educational lack.

Over three-quarters of the U.S. schools have received support from HEW, and for at least two-thirds of these schools the importance of this support has been determinant and perhaps crucial. Nonetheless, no school believes that its program would cease if government aid were reduced or cut off.

All but four of the schools which offer(ed) sixth-year programs award(ed) a certificate or degree. There are, however, almost as many different designations for the title of the award as there are awards. The disadvantages of this situation were discussed. Reference was made to the fact that specialist programs at the sixth-year level now exist in numerous other fields and are being accepted by many states as the minimum requirement for entrance into the field.

Chapter 4. The Graduates

Through the academic year 1967 - 68 fourteen schools with sixth-year programs had graduated 196 individuals; six schools had had no graduates. A questionnaire sent to 191 graduates for whom addresses were available elicited an 82.2 percent response. The statistical evidence suggests that data from the nonrespondents would not have materially altered the results.

Only about a fifth of the graduates are located in states without sixth-year program schools and, conversely, only fifteen states not having such schools have succeeded in attracting graduates of the programs; eleven of these fifteen are adjacent to states which do have schools.

The male-female ratio of graduates is almost 1:2.5. A high proportion of female graduates and a low proportion of male graduates are over forty, forty-five, and fifty years of age. Only 20 percent of the females and almost 40 percent of the males were under thirty-five.

Only a little over half of the accredited schools have supplied graduating students for the sixth-year programs and, generally speaking, the graduates have done their sixth-year work at the same school where they took their first professional degree.

Well over half of all graduates embarked upon the programs with the specific purpose of securing some kind of specialized professional education; for nearly 30 percent this specialization was library school teaching.

Sixty percent of the graduates went to the particular school they chose because of some aspect of "convenience." "Reputation of the faculty" and "reputation of the school" were given as reasons by only 12 and 16 percent, respectively, of graduates.

Library school teaching is one of the long-range career plans of nearly 40 percent of all graduates. Fewer than 30 percent of them evidenced interest in upper-level administrative responsibility of any kind.

Forty-five percent of all graduates are in college and university libraries, about 22 percent are library school teachers, and about 10 percent are employed each in public libraries, school libraries, and special libraries. Nearly 44 per-

cent of all graduates have remained in the same institution—
though not, of course, necessarily in the same position—that
they were in when they embarked upon sixth-year study.

Generally speaking, there is considerable fidelity to previous type of employment on the part of the graduates, but
the public and school libraries lost some, while library school
teaching and the academic and special libraries gained.

About 16 percent of the men and 18 percent of the women
were in the lowest salary range ($4500 - $6499) before
graduation; none had salaries this low after graduation. Only
6 percent of the men and 11 percent of the women were in
the second-lowest range after graduation, whereas before the
sixth-year program the percentages were 54 and 29, respectively. At the other end of the scale no men and only 3
percent of the women had received salaries at or above
$12,500 before taking the advanced program; after gradu-
ation 26 percent of the men and 23 percent of the women
were at this level.

Chapter 5. Evaluation

Half of 153 graduates expressed themselves as "Extremely
Satisfied" or "Well Satisfied" with their sixth-year programs;
more than three-quarters were either "Extremely Satisfied,"
"Well Satisfied," or "Content." Conversely, close to one-
quarter of all respondents were "Dissatisfied" or "Extremely
Dissatisfied." Over 80 percent of all graduates expressed
themselves as having had programs which prepared them
"Extremely Well," "Fairly Well," or "Adequately" for their
present positions, whereas about one-fifth felt themselves to
have been "Not Very Well" or "Very Poorly" prepared.

The most frequently cited suggestions and adverse criticisms from graduates were the need for: (1) more courses,
beyond the M.L.S. level, specifically for sixth-year students;
(2) improvement of the faculty; (3) updating or making more
relevant parts of the curriculum; (4) more independent or
research-oriented study; (5) more specialized courses; (6)
more course work in information science; (7) specific recognition of and reward for the sixth-year programs by libraries;
and (8) a degree or diploma as reward for satisfactory completion of the program.

Assessments of the contribution of the sixth-year programs were sought from 70 employers representing 83 graduates. Nearly half of these employers were academic librarians, and almost a fifth were library school deans. Responses were received from 64 percent of the total group.

The evaluation and assessment of these employers may be summarized as follows: (1) 16 employers, employing 18 graduates, wrote in strong, affirmative terms of the general value of the programs; (2) 19 employers, (24 graduates) believe that the *individuals* involved had been somewhat to very greatly benefited by the programs; (3) 26 employers (28 graduates) believe that the programs had been of some to "immeasurable" benefit to the *positions* the graduates held; (4) 7 employers (7 graduates) expressed doubts or little enthusiasm.

A total of 161, or almost 60 percent, of the full-time faculty of the sixth-year program schools hold no degree higher than the B.L.S./M.L.S., although many of these instructors are teaching at the sixth-year level. Very few of the sixth-year schools are employing graduates of these schools as instructors. On the other hand, nearly one-third of the full-time faculty at the schools are persons holding the doctorate, and the mean for all schools is 4.4 persons.

Based upon the findings of the report as a whole, the following conclusions are reached: (1) the basic concept of the sixth-year program is sound, and the idea should be supported and encouraged; (2) a large majority of the programs are viable, will continue, and will probably improve qualitatively and expand quantitatively; (3) a majority, probably a strong majority, of the programs are functioning reasonably well to excellently; (4) most programs can be, and a few need to be, improved in one or more respects.

Recommendations

For the reader's convenience, the principal recommendations which emerge from this study are gathered together and briefly stated here. Recommendations are given in the order in which the relevant data, or discussion, appear in the text, and the figure(s) in parentheses after each recommendation refers to the pertinent page(s).

Not all the recommendations are mathematically demonstrable and based upon quantitative findings. A few derive from correspondence, qualitative free responses to questionnaires, and discussions. No recommendation, however, represents the unsupported opinion of the investigator.

With the foregoing borne in mind it is recommended that:

1. One or two schools in the large, northwestern section of the country seriously consider the establishment of sixth-year specialist programs, especially in the areas of library school teaching, information science, the community or junior college library, and instructional materials centers (p.11, 44).

2. A year or two of professional experience generally be required for admission to any sixth-year program (p.22).

3. The fifteen schools having student attrition rates of more than 50 percent give serious consideration to this question, with the aim of reducing waste in faculty and staff time on the one hand, and of increasing the proportion of graduates who will more fully serve the profession on the other (p.30).

4. The schools, whether or not they have doctoral programs and whether or not they consider their sixth-year programs to be terminal, bear in mind, in their student counseling and in their use of research and independent study seminars, the fact that 44 percent of the present graduates viewed the programs as at least a possible first step toward the doctorate (p.32).

5. At least those schools with specializations in library school teaching make certain that their enrollees receive some exposure to the problems involved in the selection, definition, planning, and prosecution of a piece of research (p.33).

6. The Association of American Library Schools, perhaps with the aid of the C.O.A., attempt to secure agreement among the schools on not more than two or three award designations, whether

these be called certificates, diplomas, or degrees (p.35 - 36).

7. The schools which at present give no award for completion of the sixth-year programs seriously consider instituting one (p.36 - 37).

8. The schools, the programs of which have received from graduates a low proportion of satisfactory judgments or a high proportion of unsatisfactory judgments, seek to determine the causes and to provide remedies (p.64 - 65).

9. The schools spell out clearly and in detail, and put into print, the nature of their programs, what they entail, what a student may expect to secure by enrolling, and what will be expected of him (p.65).

10. Many larger libraries and most very large ones of all kinds which might beneficially employ graduates of sixth-year specialist programs establish appropriate position classifications and salary schedules (p.68).

11. The schools upgrade the educational attainment of their faculties to the end that, except under unusual and carefully evaluated circumstances, students at the sixth-year level will not be taught by instructors holding no degree higher than the B.L.S./M.L.S. (p.71 - 72).

Appendix A

<u>Accredited Library Schools</u>, Spring, <u>1969</u>

(The commonly used, abbreviated name is shown in full capitals)

ALBANY, State University of New York
School of Library Science
Albany, New York

+ATLANTA University
School of Library Service
Atlanta, Georgia

**BRITISH COLUNBIA, University of
School of Librarianship
Vancouver, British Columbia, Canada

*CALIFORNIA, University of
School of Librarianship
Berkeley, California

*CASE WESTERN RESERVE University
School of Library Science
Cleveland, Ohio

CATHOLIC University of America
Department of Library Science
Washington, D. C.

*+CHICAGO, University of
Graduate Library School
Chicago, Illinois

*+COLUMBIA University
School of Library Service
New York, New York

+DENVER, University of
Graduate School of Librarianship
Denver, Colorado

+DREXEL Institute of Technology
Graduate School of Library Science
Philadelphia, Pennsylvania

+EMORY University
Division of Librarianship
Atlanta, Georgia

*+FLORIDA State University
School of Library Science
Tallahassee, Florida

GENESEO, State University of New York,
College at, School of Library Science
Geneseo, New York

HAWAII, University of
Graduate School of Library Studies
Honolulu, Hawaii

*+ILLINOIS, University of
Graduate School of Library Science
Urbana, Illinois

*INDIANA University
Graduate Library School
Bloomington, Indiana

KANSAS State Teachers College
Department of Librarianship
Emporia, Kansas

+KENT State University
School of Library Science
Kent, Ohio

KENTUCKY, University of
Department of Library Science
Lexington, Kentucky

+LOUISIANA State University
Library School
Baton Rouge, Louisiana

McGILL University
Graduate School of Library Science
Montreal, Quebec, Canada

*+MARYLAND, University of
School of Library and Information Science
College Park, Maryland

*MICHIGAN, University of
Department of Library Science
Ann Arbor, Michigan

* +MINNESOTA, University of
Library School
Minneapolis, Minnesota

   * Offers program for doctoral degree

  ** Basic program at the fifth-year level leads to the
     professional bachelor's degree

   + Has, or has had, sixth-year specialist program
     as of August 1970

83

NORTH CAROLINA, University of
School of Library Science
Chapel Hill, North Carolina

+NORTH TEXAS State University
Department of Library Service
Denton, Texas

OKLAHOMA, University of
School of Library Science
Norman, Oklahoma

OREGON, University of
School of Librarianship
Eugene, Oregon

+PEABODY, George, College for Teachers
Peabody Library School
Nashville, Tennessee

*+PITTSBURGH, University of
Graduate School of Library
and Information Sciences
Pittsburgh, Pennsylvania

PRATT Institute
Graduate Library School
Brooklyn, New York

ROSARY College
Department of Library Science
River Forest, Illinois

*+RUTGERS University
Graduate School of Library Service
New Brunswick, New Jersey

SIMMONS College
School of Library Science
Boston, Massachusetts

*SOUTHERN CALIFORNIA, University of
School of Library Science
University Park, Los Angeles, California

*SYRACUSE University
School of Library Science
Syracuse, New York

+TEXAS, University of
Graduate School of Library Science
Austin, Texas

TEXAS WOMAN'S University
School of Library Science
Denton, Texas

**+TORONTO, University of
School of Library Science
Toronto, Ontario, Canada

+UCLA
Graduate School of Library Service
University of California at Los Angeles
Los Angeles, California

WASHINGTON, University of
School of Librarianship
Seattle, Washington

+WAYNE State University
Department of Library Science
Detroit, Michigan

+WESTERN MICHIGAN University
Department of Librarianship
Kalamazoo, Michigan

WESTERN ONTARIO, University of
School of Library and Information Science
London, Ontario, Canada

*+WISCONSIN, University of
Library School
Madison, Wisconsin

Appendix B

1. Name of school _____

2. Title of program _____

3. When was the 6th-year program begun at your School? _____

4. What is the purpose, or what are the purposes of the 6th-year program?

                                              Check those that apply:

    Specialization beyond the M.L.S.   _____

    Up-date knowledge   _____

    Upgrade professional skills   _____

    Special program for teaching librarianship   _____

    Preparation for administrative work in libraries   _____

    Information science and automation skills   _____

    Administration of instructional material centers   _____

    Other (please list): _____

    _____

    _____

    _____

    If there is available a published statement of the purpose(s) of your 6th year

    program, please include a copy.

5. Has the purpose or have these purposes of the program changed since its first

    year/first several years of operation?

        Yes _____   No _____   If yes, in what ways? _____

    _____

    _____

6. Is the 6th-year program designed as (check all that apply):

    A terminal program between the M.L.S. and the doctorate   _____

    An alternative to the doctorate   _____

    A first step toward the doctorate   _____

    No specific relationship to the doctorate   _____

    Other _____   _____

7. Development of the 6th-year program:

    a. What changes in courses and fields of specialization offered have been
        made during the years it has been in operation?

        Courses and fields added? Which? _____

        _____

        _____

        _____

        Courses and fields dropped? Which? _____

        _____

        _____

        _____

    b. What changes in the content or purposes of the 6th-year program are
        expected to be made in the next two years?

        _____

        _____

        _____

        In the next five? _____

        _____

        _____

    c. What criticisms of the program do the faculty have? (Please specify)

        _____

        _____

_____

_____

d. What criticisms of the program do the students have? (Please specify)

_____

_____

_____

_____

8. What are the admission requirements for students entering the program?

a. Master's degree from an A.L.A. accredited school?   Yes _____ No _____

b. Would a master's degree from an unaccredited school be accepted?

          Yes _____   No _____

c. Bachelor's degree in library science from an A.L.A. accredited school
(Pre-1950)?   Yes _____   No _____

d. Would undergraduate study in librarianship in conjunction with a subject
master's degree admit a student to the program?

          Yes _____   No _____

e. Would a student with an advanced degree in another field, but who did not
have a B.L.S. or M.L.S. be admitted to the program?   Yes _____ No _____

f. Is professional experience as a librarian required for admission?

          Yes _____   No _____   If yes, how many years? _____

g. Is there an age limit for admission?

          Yes _____   No _____   If yes, what? _____

h. Is a specified grade point average in prior college or university studies
required for admission?

          Yes _____   No _____   If yes, required g.p.a. _____

i. Is the Graduate Record Examination required?

          Yes _____   No _____   If yes, what score
is required for admission? _____

87

j. Other admission requirements? (<u>e.g.</u>, language, references, interview)

_____

_____

_____

9. How many students are enrolled in the current 6th-year program?

Full-time? _____   Part-time? _____   F.T.E.? _____

10. a. Please list the number of students enrolled each year since the program was initiated. (Use fall figures, <u>e.g.</u>, fall, 1960 enrollment = 1960-61 enrollment.)

	Male	Female		Male	Female		Male	Female
1960-61	___	___	1963-64	___	___	1966-67	___	___
1961-62	___	___	1964-65	___	___	1967-68	___	___
1962-63	___	___	1965-66	___	___			

b. If some students have taken the program <u>in summers only</u>, and would therefore not be included in the figures under 10a, please list the numbers here:

	Male	Female		Male	Female		Male	Female
Summer, 1960	___	___	Summer, 1963	___	___	Summer, 1966	___	___
" 1961	___	___	" 1964	___	___	" 1967	___	___
" 1962	___	___	" 1965	___	___	" 1968	___	___

11. Please list the number of students who have <u>completed</u> the program each year since it was initiated.

	Male	Female		Male	Female		Male	Female
1960	___	___	1963	___	___	1966	___	___
1961	___	___	1964	___	___	1967	___	___
1962	___	___	1965	___	___	1968	___	___

88

12. Background of students

    a. Please indicate the kinds of degrees held by the students who have completed the program since its initiation.

5th-year B.L.S.	M.L.S.	Subject Master's	Other (please specify)
Number of Male			
Number of Female			

    b. As far as possible, please indicate the total amount of library experience that students who enrolled in the 6th-year program had after their first professional degree, i.e., M.L.S., 5th-year B.L.S., etc.

No. of students	Year(s) of experience
_____	1
_____	2
_____	3
_____	4
_____	5-7
_____	8-9
_____	10-12
_____	More than 12

    c. How many students entered the 6th-year program immediately after completing the M.L.S. program? How many of these students were graduated from your library School? From another library school?

Students entering 6th-year program directly from M.L.S.

	No. from this library School	No. from another library school
1960	_____	_____
1961	_____	_____

1962 _____ _____

1963 _____ _____

1964 _____ _____

1965 _____ _____

1966 _____ _____

1967 _____ _____

1968 _____ _____

13. If student records are available on this subject, the following information would be useful concerning all students who have completed your 6th-year program:

   a. How many students completing the 6th-year program took or returned to positions in libraries? Total No. _____ In public libraries? No. _____ School libraries? No. _____ College and university libraries? No. _____ Special libraries? No. _____ Library school teaching? No. _____

   b. Of these students who completed the program, and previously held library positions, how many returned to a position in the same library? No. _____

   c. For those who have had professional library experience before completing the 6th-year program, and return to library work, are the positions they take at a higher salary than their previous one ?

Number of higher	Number of about the same (Less than $300 difference)	Number of lower	Total

   d. Do students who complete the 6th-year program directly after the M.L.S. get higher beginning salaries than do M.L.S. graduates?

Number of higher	Number of about the same (Less than $300 difference)	Number of lower	Total

14. Is a certificate or diploma awarded for successful completion of the program?

                           Yes _____   No _____

     a. If the answer is yes, what is it called? _____

     b. By whom awarded? Univ. _____ Graduate School _____ Library School _____

15. What requirements does the student have to meet to complete the program

     successfully?

     a. No. of semester units? _____   No. of semesters? _____

     b. No. of quarter units? _____   No. of quarters? _____

     c. Residence requirement? _____

     d. What grade point average has to be maintained? _____

     e. Is a thesis or research project required?   Yes _____   No _____

     f. Is there a comprehensive examination?   Yes _____   No _____

     g. Other requirements (Please specify)

         _____

         _____

         _____

16. What is the duration of the program?

        One academic year _____

        One academic year plus summer _____

        Other _____

17. Please list "fields of specialization" currently offered in the 6th-year

     curriculum:

         _____

         _____

         _____

         _____ _____

                   (Use back of page if more space is needed)

18. Please list courses <u>required</u> for all 6th-year students:

    Lecture courses: _____

    _____

    _____

    _____

    Seminars: _____

    _____

    _____

    _____

    Research courses: _____

    _____

    _____

    _____

    Tutorials: _____

    _____

    _____

    _____

    Individual project courses: _____

    _____

    _____

    _____

19. Are the courses in the curriculum exclusively for 6th-year program students?

    Yes _____ No _____; If no:

    a. Are they open to M.L.S. students? Yes _____ No _____

    b. (Where applicable) Are they open to Ph.D./D.L.S. students?

    Yes _____ No _____

20. Do courses in other fields (other departments on campus) count toward the required units for completion? Yes _____ No _____ If yes:

a. How many courses or units can be taken in other fields?

No. of courses _____   No. of Units _____

b. Are outside courses encouraged?   Yes _____   No _____

c. Are outside courses required?   Yes _____   No _____

If yes, how many courses? _____   units? _____

d. Is credit given for outside courses only in special circumstances?

Yes _____   No _____

21. Counseling and guidance

a. Is there counseling for students in the 6th-year program? Yes _____ No _____

b. Is this counseling given before enrollment?   Yes _____   No _____

During the course of the program?   Yes _____   No _____

c. Do the 6th-year students have faculty counselors?   Yes _____   No _____

22. How many courses in the 6th-year curriculum of the academic year 1968/69 are taught by the School's regular faculty members?

Total number of courses in program in 1968/69 _____

Number taught by regular faculty _____

23. Please list the part-time and/or "visiting specialist" faculty members who are teaching courses in the 1968/69 academic year (in which 6th-year students are enrolled) with current regular position and degrees held.

_____

_____

_____

_____

_____

_____

(Use back of page if more space is needed)

93

24. Were additional faculty positions added when the 6th-year program was initiated?

    Yes _____   No _____

    If yes, how many were added in F.T.E.? Number: _____

    If not, how were faculty freed to handle the program? _____

25. Is there a special faculty position budget allotment for the 6th-year program faculty, or is it part of the regular budget?

    Special budget allotment _____

    Part of regular library School budget _____

26. Does your School offer a doctoral program?   Yes _____   No _____

* 27. Is then, the 6th-year program considered a development toward offering the doctoral degree?   Yes _____   No _____

28. Whether or not your School offers the doctoral program, has the School examined the possibility of giving a M.Ph. or D. Arts degree?   Yes _____   No _____

    If it has, what part would the 6th-year curriculum play in the program of such a degree?

                                            (Check that which would apply)

    It would constitute the 1st year toward such a degree   _____

    It would constitute the entire course work for such a degree   _____

    The 6th-year program is an alternative to such a degree   _____

29. When the 6th-year program was begun, were extra budgetary provisions made for:

	Yes	No
Faculty	___	___
Other Staff	___	___
Library materials	___	___
Equipment	___	___
Extra facilities	___	___

    If not, how have the extra demands of the program been arranged?

    _____

    _____

---

* [Poorly phrased, in view of the wording of question 26. -- J.P.D.]

30. What percent of the total library School budget is allocated for or spent on the 6th-year program? % _____

31. Is there external support for the program?

   Yes _____   No _____   If yes, how much annually? _____

   a. Foundation support?

      Yes _____   No _____   If yes, how much annually? _____

   b. Federal support?

      Yes _____   No _____   If yes, how much annually? _____

      If yes, is this entirely from the provisions of Title II of the Higher Education Act?

      Yes _____   No _____   Other agency? (Please specify) _____

   c. State support?

      Yes _____   No _____   If yes, how much annually? _____

   d. Other external support? (Please specify)

      _____   How much? _____

32. Is there scholarship aid for students in the program?

   Yes _____   No _____

   a. If yes, how many students in the 1968/69 program have scholarships?

      Number _____

   b. What is the total amount of money these students receive for the academic year?

      Amount _____

   c. Where does this money come from?

      The institution   _____

      Federal funds   _____

      State funds   _____

95

33. Are there loan funds available to the 6th-year students?   Yes _____   No _____

34. If Higher Education Act, Title II funds are available to your School, and they were drastically reduced or cut off entirely, would the 6th-year program continue?

    Yes _____   No _____   Please elaborate if necessary:

    _____

    _____

    _____

35. Please supply a list of names and current addresses of students who have successfully completed the 6th-year program.

36. Please send a copy of the current school catalog, marking courses currently offered in the 6th-year program.

Thanks very much!

J.P.D.

February, 1969

Questionnaire on the Graduates of Sixth-Year Specialist Programs

April 5, 1969

Dear Colleague:

The A.L.A. Committee on Accreditation is making a comprehensive study of the nature, aims, and conditions of sixth-year, or post-M.L.S. specialist programs in A.L.A. accredited library schools. A great deal of information is being obtained from the schools. We feel, however, that an essential aspect of the investigation must be supplied by, and include evaluative opinion from those who have graduated from the programs. Consequently, we should be most grateful if you would fill out this brief questionnaire and return it in the enclosed stamped and addressed envelope. The form can be completed in fifteen minutes. The information obtained from the questionnaire will be considered strictly confidential and no individuals will be identified in the report.

We should not have agreed to undertake this study had we not been convinced that the topic is one of considerable, and increasing importance to all of us. Increasing, because the steadily enlarging demands which our very rapidly changing society is placing upon librarians and libraries inevitably call for more people with professional education beyond the M.L.S. degree. At the same time, for a majority even of upper level positions, the Ph.D. is not necessary and, in any case, the numbers of those able and willing to complete that degree will always be relatively small.

We hope you feel, as we do, that the study is needed, and that its findings will be of potential value to the profession. The study obviously cannot be as useful as it should be without your help and cooperation. These we most earnestly bespeak.

Sincerely yours,

J. Periam Danton
Professor of Librarianship

Appendix C

1. Name (may be omitted if desired) _____

2. Address _____

3. Age _____   Sex (circle one)   F   M

4. Name of library school attended for 6th-year program _____

   _____

5. Present postion: Name of institution _____

   _____

   Title of position _____

   If title is not self-explanatory, please describe your position _____

   _____

   Salary _____

6. Where and when did you obtain your B.L.S. and/or M.L.S.?

   a) Name of school(s)   B.L.S. _____ M.L.S. _____

   b) Year(s) you received B.L.S. and/or M.L.S. B.L.S. _____ M.L.S. _____

7. Do you have any other graduate degrees?   Yes _____   No _____

   If yes, please specify _____

8. Did you work as a librarian after you received the M.L.S. and before you entered the 6th-year program?

   Yes _____   No _____   If you answer No, please omit the rest of this question and questions 9 and 10.

   a) If yes, please indicate total number of years professional experience: (circle appropriate number)

       1   2   3   4   5-7   8-9   10-12   More than 12

   b) If yes, what was the position you held immediately before entering the 6th-year program?

       Name of institution _____

       Title of position _____

       If title is not self-explanatory, please describe the position _____

       _____

       Salary _____

c) If yes, please indicate your reason(s) for entering the 6th-year program:

Check those that apply:

To secure specialization beyond the M.L.S. _____

To up-date knowledge _____

To upgrade professional skills _____

For a special program for teaching librarianship _____

As preparation for administrative work _____

For Information science and automation skills _____

For administration of instructional material centers _____

As a possible step toward the doctorate _____

Other (please list): _____

_____

_____

9. If your answer to question #8 was yes, and you have returned to library work after completing the 6th-year program, is your present position at a higher salary than your previous one? (Please check appropriate box)

Higher	About the same (Less than $300 diff.)	Lower

10. If your answer to question #8 was yes, and you have returned to library work after completing 6th-year program, is your level of professional responsibility as you view it:

Higher	About the same	Lower

11. If you entered the 6th-year program immediately after receiving your M.L.S., please indicate your objective:

Check those that apply:

Because of a change in career intent _____

To secure specialization not received in the M.L.S.
program _____

99

Possible step toward doctorate _____

Other (please specify) _____

_____

12. Why did you choose this particular school?

                                        Check only those that apply:

Because same school from which you received the M.L.S.   _____

Because different from M.L.S. school   _____

Convenience - near home, job, etc.   _____

Because of the curriculum offered   _____

Reputation of the faculty   _____

Reputation of the school   _____

Reputation of the university   _____

Other (please specify): _____

_____

13. What are your long-range career plans?

Chief or assistant librarian in a major library   _____

"Middle level" administration in a major library   _____

Subject specialist in a major library   _____

Librarian in charge of a special collection, a special library (e.g., law, gov't docs., report literature, etc.)_____

Library school teaching   _____

Other (please specify): _____

_____

14. Do you feel that the 6th-year program you took prepared you for your present position? (check appropriate category):

Extremely well	Fairly well	Adequately	Not very well	Very Poorly

15. Please indicate your degree of satisfaction with the 6th-year program. (Check appropriate category):

Extremely Satisfied	Well Satisfied	Content	Dissatisfied	Extremely Dissatisfied

16. If you checked either "dissatisfied" or "extremely dissatisfied" in the previous question, please indicate here, as briefly or fully as you wish, the reasons for your dissatisfaction.

17. FINALLY! It would be much appreciated if you would tell us how you think the 6th-year program you had could be improved. Teaching quality? Teaching method? Nature of the curriculum? Appropriateness for your purpose?

Many thanks!

Appendix D

SCHOOL OF LIBRARIANSHIP
UNIVERSITY OF CALIFORNIA
BERKELEY, CALIFORNIA 94720

July 14, 1969

Dear

   As you may know, I am making a study of sixth-year specialist programs in the accredited library schools on behalf of the Committee on Accreditation of the American Library Association. We have received a great deal of information about these programs from all of the schools which have, or have had them, and from the graduates of the programs. It seems to us important that we also try to obtain from the employers of these graduates some kind of estimate or evaluation concerning the value of the additional year of study for the positions which the graduates now hold.

   I am not inflicting you with a questionnaire, but I should deeply appreciate it if you would write me in any way you wish and can on this point concerning the sixth-year program graduate(s) whose name(s) is (are) noted at the bottom of this letter. The basic question in which we are interested, and which will be of interest to the profession at large, might be phrased somewhat as follows: How useful/important/essential to the present professional activity of the graduate(s) was the additional sixth year of library school study? Or, to put it somewhat differently: Has this additional year made a difference in the manner in which, or the level at which, a graduate is able to function? In short, what we are trying to discover is something about the nature and extent of the contribution of the sixth year to librarianship, that is, to the work on the job which the graduates of the programs are performing.

   I should not have agreed to undertake this study had I not been convinced that the topic is one of considerable, and increasing importance to all of us. Increasing, because the steadily enlarging demands which our very rapidly changing society is placing upon librarians and libraries inevitably calls for more people with professional education beyond the M.L.S. degree. At the same time, for a majority even of upper level positions, the Ph.D. is not necessary and, in any case, the numbers of persons able and willing to complete this degree will always be relatively small. I hope you feel, as I do, that the study is needed and that its findings will be of potential value to the profession. The study obviously cannot be as useful as it should be without your help and cooperation. These I most earnestly bespeak.

   Let me assure you that neither your name nor the name of any graduate will be identified in the report.

   I enclose a stamped, self-addressed envelope. As we have already begun analysis of some of the data, and hope to complete the report within the next two months, I should especially appreciate hearing from you as soon as possible.

                                        Sincerely yours,

                                        J. Periam Danton
                                        Professor of Librarianship

102

Selected Bibliography

Asheim, Lester E. "Education and Manpower for Librarianship: First Steps toward a Statement of Policy," *ALA Bulletin* 62: 1096 - 1106 (October 1968).

Dalton, Jack. "Observations on Advanced Study Programs in the Library Schools of the United States," in Larry E. Bone, ed., *Library Education: An International Survey*, p.317 - 28. Urbana: Univ. of Illinois Graduate School of Library Science, 1968.

Fryden, Floyd N. "Post-Master's Degree Programs in the Accredited U.S. Library Schools," *Library Quarterly* 39: 233 - 44 (July 1969).

Fuller, Muriel. "What One Library School Has Done: A Case Study," in Guy Garrison, ed., *The Changing Role of State Library Consultants; Proceedings of a Conference Held at the University of Illinois, 26 - 29 November 1967*, p.75 - 82. Urbana: Univ. of Illinois Graduate School of Library Science, 1968. Monograph no.9.

Harrison, J. Clement. "Advanced Study: A Midatlantic View," in Larry E. Bone, ed., *Library Education: An International Survey*, p.329 - 36. Urbana: Univ. of Illinois Graduate School of Library Science, 1968.

Horn, Andrew H. ["Post-M.L.S. Certificates of Specialization in Library Science at U.C.L.A."], Letter, *AB Bookman's Weekly* 42: 1299 (21 October 1968).

Kenney, Louis A. "Continuing Education for Academic Librarians," *California Librarian* 30: 199 - 202 (July 1969).

Lowrie, Jean E. "Sixth-Year Degree," Letter, *Library Journal* 92: 170 (15 January 1967).

McKinney, Eleanor R. "Another Degree? What For?," *School Libraries* 18: 19 - 22 (Spring 1969).

"New Program [at Illinois]," *Journal of Education for Librarianship* 4: 183 - 84 (Winter 1964).

"Sixth-Year Degree Offered," *Michigan Librarian* 33: 27 - 28 (June 1967).

Swank, R. C. "Sixth-Year Curricula and the Education of Library School Faculties," *Journal of Education for Librarianship* 8: 14 - 19 (Summer 1967).